Birth of a Special Parent

-

The Path of Love, Patience, and Understanding in Raising Exceptional Children

By

Dr. Kajal Suri

(Child Psychologist and Rehabilitation Personnel)

DEDICATION

To those remarkable parents who:

- Embrace the unique journey of raising a child with special needs, transforming every challenge into a triumph of love and patience.

- Stand as pillars of unwavering strength and resilience, creating a world of possibilities for child against all odds.

- Teach us the true meaning of unconditional love and acceptance, showing that every child is a gift to be cherished.

- Inspire with their endless optimism, proving that even in the face of adversity, hope and joy can flourish.

- Share their stories and experiences, forging a community of support and understanding that uplifts every member.

- And to my own family, who has always been my source of strength and inspiration. Your love and support make everything possible.

This book is a tribute to your courage, dedication, and the beautiful journey you undertake every day.

PREFACE

As I sit down to pen the words of this book, I am acutely aware of the journey that each parent of a special needs child embarks upon - a path filled with unique challenges, profound learning, and unparalleled love. This book is born out of not just my personal experiences but also the shared stories of many such parents whose resilience and dedication have been nothing short of inspiring.

In these pages, I endeavor to offer not just insights and guidance but also a sense of camaraderie and understanding. Raising a child with special needs can often feel like navigating uncharted waters, each day bringing its own set of triumphs and trials. It is a journey that tests and reveals the depth of human strength and compassion.

This book aims to provide a comprehensive look at the various facets of this journey. From understanding the initial diagnosis to grappling with the emotional rollercoaster, from tackling the daily practicalities to celebrating the small victories that are indeed big achievements. It is a blend of practical advice, heartfelt narratives, and resources that I hope will serve as a valuable guide and companion to parents who walk this path.

I have also included personal anecdotes and experiences from other families, which I believe will resonate with many and offer the comfort that comes from knowing one is not alone in this journey. Each story, each piece of advice, is imbued with the hope and strength that characterizes special parenting.

My deepest desire is for this book to be more than just a resource; I wish for it to be a source of hope, a testament to the incredible journey of special parenthood, and a celebration of the extraordinary children who make every challenge worthwhile.

DISCLAIMER

The contents of this book, including but not limited to text, graphics, images, and other material ("Content"), are for informational purposes only. The Content is not intended to be a substitute for professional medical advice, diagnosis, or treatment. Always seek the advice of your physician or other qualified health provider with any questions you may have regarding a medical condition or the health and welfare of your child.

TABLE OF CONTENTS

*"Sometimes real superheroes live in the
hearts of small children
fighting big battles."*

BIRTH OF A SPECIAL PARENT

Psalm 127:3-5 [NIV] states, 'Children are a heritage from the Lord, offspring a reward from him. Like arrows in the hand of a warrior are children born in one's youth. Blessed is the man whose quiver is full of them. They will not be put to shame when they contend with their opponents in court.'

Jesus says, 'Children are gifts from the Lord; they are a reward from him.' The state of being a mother or a father is the most joyful feeling. Indeed, parenthood is a blessing for both father and mother. Parental love is the only love that is truly selfless and unconditional for any child. Parenthood is about accepting that you are responsible for your child's birth, education, well-being, safety, emotional maturity, and eventual achievements. A baby changes everything, creating a whole new world for both the mother and father.

As a child grows and develops, parents experience many things and help the child become an independent individual. The role of the parents becomes more crucial as the child grows. Parenting skills include offering unconditional love, validation, praise, communication, and clear boundaries. However, some children lack the abilities to grow neurotypical and understand communication. Let's first understand the difference between neurotypical and neurodivergent children.

Neurodivergent children are those whose brain processes information in a way that is different from most individuals. Children who are neurotypical develop skills such as social, organizational, or communication skills at around the same rate as others of their age. In contrast, neurodivergence is defined as a condition in an individual who is mentally disabled or has a learning disability and hence shows atypical development of behavior. Parents sometimes start to expect their child to be interested in what they want and choose the career of their choice, without realizing their capabilities. Not only the parents of special children, but all parents should embrace the real personality of their child and let go of societal pressure.

STRUGGLES OF BEING A SPECIAL PARENT

Every child is unique, possessing their own strengths and weaknesses. Their development progresses according to these attributes during their developmental years. When a child is diagnosed with developmental delay or a disability such as a learning disability, autism, or a physical disability, parents may experience a range of emotions, including sadness and a sense of grief. The birth of a special parent—someone who raises a child with special needs—often brings numerous challenges, including social isolation, emotional stress, and financial problems. A special child may face delays in speech, mobility, socialization, or academics. Consequently, the life of a special parent is often filled with challenges and struggles. It's not surprising that parents of children with special needs experience higher levels of emotional stress compared to other parents. This stress can include insecurities about parenting competence, grief for the future they had anticipated for their child, and dealing with the specific needs of a special child. Financial stress begins with paying for psychologist visits, speech therapists, and occupational therapists, depending on the child's needs. Depending on the level of the child's disability, parenting can become more than a full-time job.

Among the many challenges, the most demanding is learning about the disability, researching, and finding effective treatments and therapies. Parents should first focus on understanding the condition. Learning everything about your child's condition can help in identifying potential treatments and therapies. Encourage age-appropriate and ability-appropriate education plans for your child, as this can be therapeutic for them. Education is one way to progress a child's brain development.

Special needs children may require extra support, such as additional classes or therapy sessions, but it can be very fruitful if parents themselves learn about all the programs suitable for their child. Raising a child with special needs is challenging. Every child with a disability also has strengths. These may be in art, music, dance, or playing an instrument. It's important for parents to focus on what their children can do according to their abilities, rather than just fretting about their disabilities.

To overcome stress and attain optimum mental peace while raising a child with special needs, parents must practice positive affirmations. Be kind to yourself and remind yourself that you are doing the best you can. Parents should take care of themselves and keep healthy. Connecting with other parents in similar situations can be helpful. Talking to people who understand what it's like to have a child with special needs can provide support. Raising a child with special needs is particularly challenging when others do not understand the issues. Most experts believe that developmental disabilities can improve as children get older. There are several things you can do as a parent to ensure that your child has the happiest, most meaningful, and healthiest future possible with all the advocacy and home remedial plans discussed in this book. The event of a child being born with a disability is always a tragedy for the parent, but early intervention and support may help the parent become positively involved in the care and development of the child with special needs. It's not the birth of a special child, but the birth of a special parent that helps the child overcome the challenges and struggles associated with the condition and live life in a miraculous way.

ABOUT THE BOOK

This book reviews literature on various disabilities, detailing their signs and symptoms, assessments, and evaluations that can be conducted at home. It provides information on how to implement various therapies and home remedial plans, making it a valuable resource for parents of children with developmental delays such as ADHD, autism, and related behavioral issues. 'Birth of a Special Parent' is the story of a parent who becomes their child's best advocate over time.

The book emphasizes that love is paramount when a child looks up to their parents. It advises against labeling the child and encourages patience and understanding in communication. It cautions parents and other family members against making hurtful remarks, underlining the importance of a nurturing environment.

This guide contains numerous tips for raising a child with special needs and includes information about speech delay, ADHD, dyslexia, dysgraphia, dyscalculia, autism, and Down syndrome. It provides methods to assess a child's IQ at home, understand their condition, create effective individual education plans, and offers remedial plans and worksheets.

By reading this book, parents can equip themselves with the skills to become home therapists. It reminds parents of the importance of self-care and mental health, as the journey can be long and demanding. Readers will learn to embrace their multiple roles - as a therapist, educator, psychologist, and most importantly, as a parent. The book encourages taking time to appreciate the child's uniqueness and loving them in the way only a parent can."

Dr. Kajal Suri

THE CHILD WITH DISABILITIES

When a baby comes into the world, it is a cause for great celebration. It's a celebration of life, dreams, hope, and possibilities. However, the birth of a child with disabilities often brings disappointment and social challenges for the parents, leading to a process of denial and grief. These children may have special needs due to a syndrome, physical disability, profound cognitive impairment, or associated disorders. Others may have specific learning disabilities, global developmental delays, or intellectual disabilities.

The World Health Organization (WHO) defines impairment as any loss or abnormality of psychological, physiological, or anatomical structure. Often, impairment can be corrected or its effects reduced with the help of technology and therapy. An impairment becomes a disability when it develops to the extent that the individual cannot fully participate in social and vocational areas. Despite the Constitution of India guaranteeing equality to all citizens, children with disabilities often face stigma, discrimination, and neglect due to social and cultural reasons, compounded by stereotypical attitudes and negative perceptions.

The Rights of Persons with Disabilities Act 2016 in India includes 21 conditions under the category of disability, aiding the inclusion of children with special needs in the general education system. This law allows children with disabilities to access quality and free primary and secondary education on an equal basis with other children in their community. The Act covers various disabilities discussed in the book, including autism spectrum disorder, specific learning disorders, intellectual disability, cerebral palsy, visual impairment, and hearing impairment.

Children's most critical cognitive development occurs during their preschool years. Therefore, early intervention programs, designed for children up to 6 years of age, are crucial for their optimum development in areas like speech, social skills, and communication. These programs include therapeutic services by specialists such as speech pathologists and occupational therapists. Parents play a vital role in these programs as the primary providers of their child's developmental needs. Children's learning occurs during daily routine activities in their home environment, and early intervention programs maximize these learning opportunities. Play therapy, including structured and routine activities, is essential for children with autism spectrum disorders and global developmental delays. It addresses behavior issues, teaches social skills, and assists in coping with challenging situations. Parents can learn various play therapies to conduct at home, such as physical plays, dramatic plays, sensory plays, music therapy, and art therapy.

Many children with disabilities are capable of reading, writing, and solving mathematical problems. The need of the hour is to support them so their disability does not render them handicapped, enabling them to be considered integral parts of society.

STORY OF A SPECIAL PARENT

When Shubh, the first boy child in their clan, was born, his family celebrated with great joy, distributing sweets throughout the area. He was adored by his grandparents and other family members in their joint family of six. However, his grandparents, both over 70, could not be very involved with him. Shubh's older sister, a 9th-grade student, and he formed a close sibling bond. Shubh, being the youngest and second in birth order, received ample pampering, especially from his mother.

Shubh's father, a commerce graduate, is preoccupied with his business, while his mother, Shree, a postgraduate, is a housewife. At 10 years old, Shubh was diagnosed with mild intellectual disabilities, significantly impacting Shree's life. Shree, previously employed since her marriage, had to leave her job seven years ago upon realizing Shubh's condition. Concerns arose when Shubh didn't learn to walk by age 3 and showed speech delays and unresponsiveness to stimuli. After medical consultations, it was confirmed that Shubh was a special child. This revelation brought worry and solemnity to the parents, especially Shree, who faced sleepless nights pondering her next steps.

As a lower-middle-class family with limited resources, Shree felt helpless and sought further suggestions. With her husband engrossed in work, Shree decided to leave her job to focus on Shubh. She struggled with loneliness and helplessness, noticing Shubh's inability to understand anything at age 4 due to speech delay. Despite trying various treatments and therapies, progress was slow, leading Shree into depression and anxiety, and she struggled to care for their elder daughter.

At a point of near hopelessness, Shree met an acquaintance who suggested training Shubh at home. She decided to use her observational skills and the internet to aid Shubh's speech and cognitive development. Shree utilized creative materials at home, flashcards, and reinforcement materials, and involved the grandparents in reading sessions with Shubh. She also took him for occupational therapy to improve his motor skills. Within eight to nine months, Shubh began walking independently and developed a vocabulary of 50 to 60 words. Shree established a 40-minute physical exercise routine with Shubh and his father and gave Shubh nightly massages to strengthen his joints.

Shubh showed tremendous improvement, eventually managing his daily routine activities with some independence. Shree's efforts led to his admission to school at age 6. Initially, his communication skills were poor, and he struggled with making friends, but he gradually became more active and talkative. Shree maintained clear communication and set strict rules, including nightly counseling sessions with Shubh to discuss his day and behaviors.

In academics, Shubh faced challenges, especially with written assessments and comprehension in class 4. Shree worked closely with his teacher, implementing a buddy system and creating worksheets at different levels to aid his learning. She also used graphic organizers and mind maps to simplify chapter learning. By the end of the year, Shubh showed improvements in motor coordination and letter formation.

I met Shree during her search for therapists and special educators. With my guidance on home remedial plans, she could conduct special education sessions for Shubh at home. Her positive attitude and practice in responding to Shubh's needs were admirable. Parenting, especially as a special parent, requires immense patience and discipline. It's crucial to regulate emotions and avoid negative disciplining methods. Positive parenting involves a firm attitude, setting clear rules, and understanding the child's capabilities and needs. The goal is to raise happy, responsible individuals, celebrating every small success and improvement. Being a special parent is an extraordinary journey, and it's important to practice daily positive affirmations and count blessings, recognizing that everyone faces their own battles.

HAPPY PARENTS, HAPPY KIDS!

Raising a child with special needs is an inherently challenging journey, as it demands a higher level of support and care. No amount of preparation can truly prepare you for this experience; what makes the greatest difference is training your own mind and cultivating a positive attitude. The grief that often accompanies each hospital visit is profound, and words barely do it justice. Accepting that your child is different or disabled is one of the most difficult aspects of being a parent. As harsh as it may sound, the sooner this acceptance settles in, the easier your journey as a special parent will become. When faced with troubles, it's natural for human beings to yearn for escape and seek a more pleasant life elsewhere. Yet, true happiness isn't found in external surroundings; it's discovered within our hearts by nurturing a positive mindset.

Becoming a positive and happy parent is a gradual process, requiring significant self-care and self-motivation. Parenting is like a roller coaster ride, full of ups and downs. Parenting special needs children demands both physical and mental effort. During moments of self-doubt and self-judgment, it's vital for parents to pause and reflect on their achievements, recognizing and valuing them.

Parents should focus on their core values, using them as a guiding force in challenging situations. Let these values be the foundation of your family, helping you determine what is truly important and what can wait. Each child, and consequently each parent, is unique. By parenting a special child, you transform into a special parent, with your value system as your beacon. Our styles of handling situations and problems aren't innate; they are shaped by our childhood experiences, the environments we've been part of, and our daily definitions of happiness and success. Strive to create a safe and happy environment for your child and family, free from the pressures of social judgments and expectations. Remember, you are parenting the child you have, not the child you might have wished for.

GLOBAL DEVELOPMENTAL DELAYS

Global Developmental Delay (GDD) is a condition that manifests during a child's developmental period, affecting crucial milestones such as crawling, walking, communication, and socialization. This delay, often apparent in the first few years of life, impacts major areas of a child's development, especially communication and social skills. Children with GDD may exhibit a diffused distribution of neurons in the brain. The term is typically used to describe delays in children from birth to 18 years old. GDD can be caused by various factors, including premature birth, chromosomal conditions like Fragile X syndrome, metabolic conditions such as thyroid issues, and brain injuries or infections like head injuries or meningitis.

<u>Signs and Symptoms of Global Developmental Delay include:</u>

1. **Speech and Language:** If a child struggles with understanding spoken language or following directions by the age of 2, it could indicate a delay. They might have limited vocabulary compared to peers or difficulties with pronunciation and articulation. In such cases, consulting a professional speech pathologist is advisable.

2. **Motor Skills:** Signs of delay in motor skills include difficulties with movements such as crawling, walking,

jumping, or balancing at the age of 2. If a child struggles with holding objects, using utensils, or manipulating small items, it's important to seek the opinion of a healthcare specialist.

3. **Social Skills:** Difficulty in forming eye contact, understanding or expressing emotions by the age of 2 can be a sign of delay. Such children might also exhibit behavioral problems like aggression or withdrawal and face challenges in maintaining peer relationships.

4. **Cognitive Skills:** Poor attention span and difficulty in remembering information at the age of 2, or challenges with problem-solving or logical thinking by the age of 4, are indicative of cognitive delays.

5. **Adaptive Functioning Skills:** If a child has difficulties with self-help skills such as dressing, feeding, or toileting by the age of 5, it suggests a delay in adaptive functioning. This may lead to struggles with daily routines and adapting to new skills.

Parents and caregivers who notice these signs in their children should seek professional guidance to understand the nature of the delay and explore appropriate interventions.

How To Outgrow Developmental Delay?

Developmental delay can be isolated, meaning it affects only one area of a child's development. This often implies that the child is developing a particular skill slower than their peers. Most developmental delays, especially isolated ones, can resolve over time with early intervention programs and therapies, enabling children to catch up to their peers and reach their full potential. However, if significant delays occur in two or more areas of development, the child may be experiencing Global Developmental Delay. For some children, developmental delays are short-term and can improve with support in physiotherapy and occupational therapy. For others, the delay is due to a learning disability, indicating that the child's brain functions differently from other children, often resulting in lifelong conditions.

It's important to distinguish between developmental delays and developmental disabilities. Developmental disabilities, such as Autism Spectrum Disorder, are different from developmental delays. Unlike delays, developmental disabilities like autism do not resolve on their own and are usually lifelong conditions requiring ongoing support and therapies. Autism is a neurodevelopmental disorder that is present from early childhood.

Developmental screening can be an effective tool to assess if a child is acquiring age-appropriate basic skills. Unlike other medical conditions, there are no laboratory or blood tests to determine developmental delays. However, the Indian Scale of Assessment of Autism is a specific test for screening autism. Parents can also find developmental screening tools online to track their child's progress in achieving milestones. These milestones range from birth to 4 years of age and include physical achievements like neck holding, sitting, standing, crawling, walking, and hopping on one foot, as well as speech and language milestones like saying words, asking questions, understanding phrases, and following instructions.

If parents observe delays in two or more milestones, they should immediately consult a pediatrician or healthcare provider. It's important to note that there is a wide range of normal development and behavior, and it's natural for children to reach certain milestones earlier or later than the general trend. In some cases, a child may have achieved all age-appropriate milestones and been admitted to preschool, yet still struggle with self-help skills such as toileting habits or managing personal belongings like bags and books.

AUTISM SPECTRUM DISORDER

Autism Spectrum Disorder (ASD) is a developmental disability stemming from structural or chemical differences in the brain. As a neurodevelopmental disorder, it significantly impacts the nervous system, affecting the cognitive, emotional, social, and physical health of the affected individual. ASD encompasses a diverse range of conditions, characterized by varying degrees of difficulty in social interaction, communication, and sometimes, the presence of highly unusual behavior and multiple problems. Being an umbrella term, the range and severity of symptoms can vary widely among individuals. For instance, while some children with autism are non-speaking, others may have proficient spoken language. Autism is typically diagnosed before the age of 3 years and significantly impairs a person's ability to communicate, understand relationships, and relate to others. The following are signs and symptoms that parents should watch for to determine if their child may have ASD:

1. Speech and Language: Some children with autism are non-speaking, while others have proficient language skills. A notable symptom is echolalia, where the child repeats words or phrases, such as repeating a question rather than answering it.

2. Eye Contact: Children on the autism spectrum often have difficulty making or sustaining eye contact. They might experience sensory overload and use excess blinking as a way to regulate sensory input.

3. Social Communication and Interaction: These children may struggle with social interaction, failing to understand others' body language. They often have difficulties playing with peers, as they might not understand how to wait, take turns, or follow game rules.

4. Sensory Issues: Children with ASD might display compulsive tendencies towards senses like smell or touch, resist cuddling, and retreat into their own world. They can be hypersensitive to bright lights, sounds, smells, textures, and tastes, leading to sensory avoidance and specific food preferences.

5. Patterns of Behavior: Repetitive motor mannerisms, such as rocking, spinning, hand flapping, or finger flipping, are common. These children may exhibit odd movement patterns, like clumsiness or walking on toes, and have stiff or exaggerated body language. They often show resistance to change and insist on sameness.

6. Stimming: Stimming refers to self-stimulating behaviors, often involving repetitive motions or sounds. While stimming associated with autism isn't always a cause for concern, it becomes an issue if it interferes with learning, results in social exclusion, or is destructive.

Parents and caregivers who notice these signs should consult a healthcare professional for a thorough evaluation and appropriate intervention strategies.

<u>Causes of Autism Spectrum Disorder:</u>

The exact cause of Autism Spectrum Disorder (ASD) is not yet fully understood. However, several risk factors have been identified. These include certain genetic mutations, genetic disorders like Fragile X syndrome, and environmental factors such as exposure to heavy metals and other toxins. While there is some evidence suggesting a genetic component to ASD, it is not considered the sole cause. Additionally, maternal alcohol or drug abuse during pregnancy has been identified as a potential risk factor for autism.

<u>Living with Autism:</u>

Children with ASD often have the capability to read, write, and solve mathematical problems. They can attend college and pursue careers of their choice. Early intervention programs and therapies can significantly help these neurodivergent children. For some with mild ASD, symptoms may improve with age, leading to increased social engagement and fewer behavioral disturbances. Many children with autism excel academically, aided by their strong memory skills. With proper training in behavior management, they can successfully attend school. ABA (Applied Behavior Analysis) therapy plans are often beneficial, as many children with ASD respond well to visual learning styles. Parents and therapists can collaboratively design activities and self-help skill programs tailored to the child's natural home environment. It's important to note that the life expectancy for individuals with autism varies widely and is influenced by various factors, including associated health conditions.

<u>Treatments and Therapies for Autism:</u>

Currently, there is no specific medication or treatment that cures ASD. However, certain physical or medical issues associated with autism may require medication. Treatment for autism primarily involves therapies that address specific symptoms and support development. These include speech therapy, occupational therapy, physical therapy, and behavioral therapies like ABA. Each therapy plan is typically customized to meet the individual needs of the child with autism.

<u>Home Remedial Plan</u>

ABA (Applied Behavior Analysis) is a highly effective therapy and intervention program, specifically structured and specialized to meet the needs of children with Autism Spectrum Disorder (ASD).   It can be effectively implemented by parents at home, as it is based on routine-based planning.   This guidance will help you understand how to apply ABA therapy at home to assist your child in learning new skills and reducing undesired behaviors.   ABA therapy is founded on the principles of behavioral science and focuses on understanding how people learn, behave, and change.   It has been shown to yield remarkable results in children on the autism spectrum.   ABA strategies are beneficial not only for children with disabilities, including ASD, but also for those without.   They can be used for teaching basic tasks like doing homework, cleaning up a room, taking a shower, or brushing teeth, as well as addressing more significant concerns like aggressive behavior or repetitive motor mannerisms.

<u>ABA therapy includes the following key strategies:</u>

1.   Positive Reinforcement: This involves adding a stimulus—an activity or item—immediately after a desired behavior is exhibited, which increases the likelihood of the behavior recurring in the future.   For example, if a child with autism cleans their room without being asked and receives a chocolate or candy as a reward, they are more likely to repeat the behavior. Reinforcers can vary, including activities like board games, video games, or outdoor play, and not just edible items.

2. Operant Extinction: It's important to understand the difference between operant extinction and classical extinction as both play a role in behavior modification in children with autism. Classical extinction involves weakening or eliminating a conditioned response by repeatedly presenting the conditioned stimulus without the unconditioned stimulus. In contrast, operant extinction involves the weakening or cessation of a voluntary or conditioned response. For instance, if a child associates the sound of a microwave with getting popcorn and then experiences several instances where the microwave is used without making popcorn, they may gradually stop responding to the sound.

3. Providing Prompt: A prompt can be an object, an item, or an action that effectively encourages a response from the child. Prompts are antecedents, meaning they are given before the desired behavior is expected to start. Using a prompt is unnecessary if the child is already completing the task through positive reinforcement. The types of prompts include:

- **Verbal Prompt:** This involves giving the child a verbal cue or instruction.

- **Gestural Prompt:** Any gesture, such as nodding the head or pointing to an object, serves as a gestural prompt and can also be a visual cue.

- **Modeling Prompt:** This requires the parent to first demonstrate the task, then ask the child to replicate it.

- **Physical Prompt:** This type of prompt involves providing guided physical assistance to help the child complete the task.

- **Visual Prompt:** A visual prompt uses pictures, photographs, videos, or other visual cues.

- **Positional Prompt:** This involves placing the correct response or item near the child to encourage the desired action.

4. Behavior Modeling: Behavior modeling is an effective method for teaching various skills to children with autism. It involves the following steps:

- **Description:** Describe to the child the expected behavior in a structured manner.

- **Modeling:** Display or model the effective use of these behaviors for the child.

- **Implementation:** Provide opportunities and an appropriate environment for the child to practice these behaviors.

5. Clear and Consistent Rules: It is essential to maintain routines for children on the autism spectrum. Clearly define your goals and communicate the rules to the child. Creating a daily routine that aligns with these goals and consistently following it is crucial. Understanding what is expected and having clear rules provide a roadmap for disciplined action.

6. Teaching Skills through Shaping: When shaping a behavior, start with small steps. As the child improves at each step, incrementally increase the complexity. This process is repeated until the child masters the behavior."

These strategies are foundational in ABA therapy, providing a structured approach to support the development and behavior management of children with ASD.

Sensory Integration Therapy

Sensory Integration Therapy is designed for children on the autism spectrum who struggle with sensory processing, helping them to effectively interpret and respond to different sensory inputs like touch, smell, taste, sight, and hearing. This therapy is typically conducted by specially trained occupational therapists in clinical settings. However, parents can also facilitate play-oriented sessions at home using equipment such as swings, trampolines, and slides.

To alleviate sensory overload, deep pressure joint exercises are beneficial for children with ASD. Activities involving swings, trampolines, and large balls provide essential sensory input. Swinging and spinning, in particular, are used to offer vestibular input, which is crucial for balance and movement.

The core theory of Sensory Integration Therapy is to comprehend behavior and devise interventions that address specific sensory issues impacting functional performance. This therapy is believed to improve challenging or repetitive behaviors in children with ASD. Body massages and pressure can soothe the joints, while oral stimulation can be provided through facial massage or brushing inside the mouth. Both hot and cold packs applied to the cheeks can also be beneficial.

Creating a tactile sensory corner at home can stimulate under-responsive children. This corner can be outfitted with soft furnishings and a variety of textures, like grass carpets, soft fur toys, and rough-surfaced mats. Some children might find solace in a secluded tent within this sensory space. This corner can serve as a calming area for overstimulated children or as a stimulating environment for those who seek more sensory input.

Music therapy is another effective component of Sensory Integration Therapy. Soft, soothing instrumental music can be played, and keeping headphones in the sensory corner can be helpful. Dancing to music is also a form of movement therapy, aiding children in achieving emotional, cognitive, physical, and social integration.

Screening Recommendations

Research indicates that Autism Spectrum Disorder (ASD) can sometimes be detected as early as 18 months. By the age of 3, a diagnosis made by an experienced professional can be considered very reliable. However, many children do not receive a formal diagnosis until they are much older. The American Academy of Pediatrics recommends that all children be screened for developmental delays and disabilities during regular doctor visits from the age of 9 months to 30 months. Parents can also assess their child at home using tools like the Indian Scale of Assessment of Autism. While there is no cure for Autism, early intervention can significantly impact the development of a child with ASD, making a substantial difference in their progress and quality of life.

ATTENTION DEFICIT HYPERACTIVITY DISORDER

ADHD (Attention Deficit Hyperactivity Disorder) is one of the most common neurodevelopmental disorders in childhood. Typically first diagnosed in childhood, it often continues into adulthood. Children with ADHD may struggle with maintaining attention, controlling impulsive behaviors, or may be excessively active. They often act without considering the consequences. Some children with ADHD exhibit milder symptoms, such as being overly active and having difficulty focusing on tasks, which can lead to issues with self-esteem and social functioning.

ADHD is often first noticed in children between one and a half to 2 years old, especially if they have speech delays, poor eye contact, or other developmental concerns. It is also identified in school-aged children when it leads to classroom disruptions or problems with schoolwork. ADHD is more commonly diagnosed in boys than in girls. It may coexist with other mental health conditions, such as anxiety disorders, autism, and learning disorders.

The exact cause of ADHD is still unknown, but there is growing evidence suggesting a genetic component. Studies have shown anatomical differences in the brains of children with ADHD compared to those without the condition. These differences include reduced volumes of gray and white matter and varied brain region activations during certain tasks.

Parents can implement behavior training for children with ADHD in a home environment. Students whose learning is impaired may qualify for special education services under the Individuals with Disabilities Education Act. Children with ADHD can benefit from study skills instruction, changes to classroom setup, alternative teaching techniques, and a modified curriculum.

ADHD (Attention Deficit Hyperactivity Disorder) presents with the following symptoms and patterns:

1. **Inattention:** This involves difficulties in maintaining focus on one task, sustaining attention, and staying organized. These issues arise not from a lack of understanding but from a deficit in concentration.

2. **Hyperactivity:** Children exhibiting hyperactivity may seem to be in constant motion, even in inappropriate situations. They might be excessively fidgety or talk non-stop. A hallmark of this symptom is a significant level of restlessness.

3. Impulsivity: Impulsivity in ADHD manifests as acting without forethought or having difficulty with self-control. This might include a desire for immediate rewards or an inability to delay gratification. Impulsive children may interrupt others frequently or make important decisions without considering the long-term consequences.

Treatment

Treating ADHD typically involves a combination of therapy and medication. For school-aged children and younger, psychostimulants such as amphetamines and methylphenidate are often the first-line pharmaceutical treatments for managing ADHD symptoms. However, it's generally recommended that these medications be reserved for cases of severe ADHD or significant behavioral issues. Current guidelines suggest that methylphenidate may be preferable to amphetamines, particularly if behavioral interventions alone are not sufficiently effective in managing the symptoms.

Home Remedial Plan

PARENT CHILD INTERACTION THERAPY

Parent-Child Interaction Therapy (PCIT) is an evidence-based treatment in America for young children with behavioral issues, grounded in Baumrind's [1966] developmental theory of parenting. PCIT merges elements of love, nurturance, effective communication, and firm control. It typically involves coaching sessions where the parent and child are in a playroom, and a therapist observes their interactions through a one-way mirror or via a live video call. This allows the therapist to provide real-time coaching on skills to manage the child's behavior. We offer insights on how parents can implement PCIT at home using playful methods. PCIT is structured into two treatment phases:

1. **Establishing a Warm Relationship:** The first phase focuses on fostering warmth in the parent-child relationship. This involves learning and applying skills that help children feel calm, secure, and positive about themselves in relation to their parents. Before starting direct interaction, parents should establish rapport with the child for about 15 days. Daily sessions of 30-40 minutes, involving board games, watching videos, or other enjoyable activities, are recommended. Parents should talk about their child's strengths, expressing fondness and appreciation for their character traits.

2. **Managing Challenging Behaviors:** The second phase addresses managing challenging behaviors while maintaining confidence, calmness, and consistency in discipline. The actual therapy begins when parents apply

proven strategies to help the child understand their limits and adapt to new behavior modifications.

PCIT aids in fostering positive interactions between parents and children and trains parents in implementing consistent, non-violent discipline techniques. It is based on both attachment and social learning principles and advocates for an authoritative style of parenting, which encompasses love, effective communication, and firm control.

INTELLECTUAL DISABILITY

Intellectual disability, historically referred to as mental retardation, is distinct from mental illness. Unlike mental illness, which can often be treated and resolved, intellectual disability is a lifelong condition. It involves a discrepancy between mental and physical development, rather than a psychological disturbance that could be treated medically. Children with mental illnesses typically experience normal development but suffer from psychological issues that require medical treatment and systemic therapies.

In contrast, intellectual disability is characterized by limitations in intellectual functioning and adaptive behavior, affecting social and practical skills. This condition is lifelong, but it is important to recognize that individuals with intellectual disabilities possess the potential to be trained and can become independent to varying degrees. With appropriate support and training, many people with intellectual disabilities can lead fulfilling and productive lives.

According to the World Health Organization (WHO), intellectual disability is characterized by a significantly reduced ability to understand new or complex information and to learn and apply new skills. This results in a diminished capacity for independent coping and typically begins before adulthood, with a lasting impact on development. Intellectual disability involves impairments in general mental abilities affecting functioning in two key areas:

1. Intellectual Functioning: Intellectual functioning is measured using psychometrically valid intelligence tests. While a specific full-scale IQ test score is not solely required for diagnosis, it can indicate significant limitations in intellectual functioning. A full-scale IQ score around 70-75 is often associated with intellectual disability. However, scores on various subtests can vary, making the full-scale IQ score an important but not exclusive indicator of overall intellectual functioning and areas that may require more attention. Therefore, clinical judgment from a registered psychologist is highly recommended for interpreting IQ test results.

2. Adaptive Functioning: Adaptive functioning encompasses three primary areas:

- **Conceptual Skills:** This includes language, reading, writing, and math skills, as well as reasoning, knowledge, problem-solving, and memory.

- **Social Skills:** This encompasses empathy, social judgment, communication skills, understanding and following rules, and the ability to make and sustain friendships.

- **Practical Skills:** This area covers skills needed for independent living, such as personal care, job responsibilities, managing money, recreation, and organizing school and work tasks."

Identification Of Mental Retardation

Mild Intellectual Disability: An IQ score ranging from 50 to 69 is indicative of mild intellectual disability. Individuals with this level of disability often experience delayed language understanding and use, as well as executive speech problems. These challenges can affect their development towards independence.

Moderate Intellectual Disability: An IQ score between 35 and 49 signifies moderate intellectual disability. Language development in affected individuals varies significantly. Some may engage in simple conversations, while others may have limited language abilities primarily used to communicate basic needs.

Severe Intellectual Disability: An IQ score from 20 to 34 points to severe intellectual disability. Individuals in this category typically exhibit marked motor impairments or other deficiencies, indicative of significant damage or maldevelopment of the central nervous system.

Profound Intellectual Disability: An IQ score below 20 is associated with profound intellectual disability. Most individuals with this level of disability have severe mobility restrictions or are immobile and are incapable of verbal communication. They possess minimal to no ability to care for their basic needs and require constant assistance and supervision.

Special Education For ID

Special education is the practice of tailoring educational approaches to meet the unique needs of children with intellectual disabilities. It acknowledges and accommodates their individual differences, disabilities, and special requirements. Due to challenges in cognitive abilities and slower physical and mental activities, children with intellectual disabilities may struggle with recognizing common shapes and symbols. Thus, special education involves specially designed, carefully planned, and meticulously monitored teaching procedures. These are essential to equip individuals with the skills necessary for independent functioning in their daily lives. The National Institute for the Mentally Handicapped (NIMH) provides a comprehensive manual on functional academics specifically for students with intellectual disabilities.

<u>Functional Academics</u>

Functional Academics primarily focuses on teaching functional reading, writing, and arithmetic. The term 'functional' pertains to the application of learned skills in real-world, community settings, tailored to individual needs.

1. Teaching Functional Reading: This process involves a variety of strategies to meet the unique needs of students with intellectual disabilities. The primary goal, especially for students with mild to moderate disabilities, is to develop the ability to read for protection and survival. Another important objective is reading for information and instructions, enabling individuals to understand job applications, newspaper advertisements, and telephone directories.

Here are insights into how functional reading can be effectively taught to children with intellectual disabilities:

- **Sight Word Vocabulary:** Teaching sight words can be approached through various methods, including imagery. Words can be categorized into high and low imagery. High imagery words are usually concrete and can include nouns like 'ball', 'mango', 'fan', and 'car'. In contrast, low imagery words are often abstract, such as adjectives like 'beautiful', 'fast', and 'good'. Parents should select words that are frequently used at home or in school, beginning with pairing activities that use pictures with words. Start with two pictures and their corresponding names for pairing, gradually increasing the number as the student progresses.

These methods aim to make reading a practical and accessible skill for students with intellectual disabilities, enhancing their ability to navigate and interact with their community effectively.

Errorless Discrimination: Errorless teaching is an instructional strategy designed to ensure that children always respond correctly. As each skill is taught, children are provided with a prompt or cue immediately following an instruction, thereby reducing or virtually eliminating the chances of incorrect responses. This gradual training procedure minimizes errors and can be implemented using flashcards or matching board games. For example, in a matching task for the spelling of 'apple' and its corresponding picture, the exercise might include more pictures of apples than other objects. Similarly, there could be more spellings of 'apple' alongside various pictures to match.

2. Teaching Functional Writing: To teach functional writing, students typically go through a six-step process that incorporates auditory, visual, tactile, and kinesthetic inputs:

1. The teacher says the word, and the student repeats it.

2. The meaning of the word is discussed and taught.

3. The word's configuration is drawn.

4. The actual word is traced or written by the student.

5. The student articulates the sound of each letter while tracing the word.

6. Once the child consistently copies the word without errors, the next step is to encourage writing from memory.

3. Teaching Functional Mathematics: Functional mathematics covers pre-computational skills such as understanding the concept of quantity, numbers, and counting. Once the child grasps these foundational concepts, more complex computational skills like addition, subtraction, multiplication, and division can be introduced. Periodic tests can help parents assess the child's comprehension. Subsequently, cognitive skills involving the application of concepts like money, time, weight, and distance can be taught. Children with mild to moderate intellectual disabilities may be capable of solving word problems that require reading, understanding, and applying appropriate computation.

For Those Who Cannot Read And Write

For children with mild and moderate intellectual disabilities, who may struggle with abstract concepts and symbols, alternative skills focusing on daily, weekly, monthly, and occasional needs can be taught. This need-based training is vital for helping them function independently in the community. Here are some suggested steps to guide parents in this process:

Daily Needs:

- Bathing

- Brushing teeth

- Dressing

- Toileting

Weekly Needs:

- Washing clothes

- Visiting a place of worship

- Ironing clothes

Monthly Needs:

- Buying groceries and other provisions

- Paying the electricity bill

- Visiting relatives

Occasional Needs:

- Going to a movie

- Celebrating festivals

- Attending weddings or parties

By focusing on these areas, parents can equip their children with the necessary skills to manage everyday tasks and participate in community life more effectively.

Home Remedial Plan

ACTIVITIES OF DAILY LIVING

Activities of Daily Living, commonly referred to as ADLs, are basic, everyday tasks that include eating, bathing, dressing, and toileting. While most children learn these tasks relatively easily and incorporate them into their daily routines, children with special needs may find these tasks more challenging and might require consistent training to complete them. For instance, a child with motor difficulties may find an activity like buttoning a sweater very challenging. Additionally, children with social interaction difficulties may lack motivation to perform certain activities that their peers do, affecting their ability to live independently.

Parents play a crucial role in enhancing the ADL skills of their special needs children, especially in their early years. Through targeted efforts, parents can help their children become physically, psychologically, and socially independent. For example, children who struggle with brushing their teeth or taking showers can benefit from step-by-step training. This process involves breaking down each activity into smaller, manageable steps. For brushing teeth, these steps could include reaching for the toothbrush, grasping it, picking it up, and beginning to brush. Similarly, for taking a shower, the process might be divided into removing clothes, reaching for the soap, applying the soap, and starting the shower.

All self-care tasks like eating, dressing, toilet hygiene, and personal grooming can be taught using this method. To aid in this process, parents can place pictures illustrating different activities and their steps on the walls of relevant areas. For example, a picture in the bathroom might show the steps for taking a shower, with an arrow pointing to where the soap is kept. Similarly, a visual guide for hand washing could depict a four-step process and be placed on the wall near the sink.

These visual aids and step-by-step approaches can significantly assist children with special needs in mastering essential life skills for daily living.

VISUAL IMPAIRMENT

According to the World Health Organization (WHO), visual impairment and blindness are defined based on specific criteria. Blindness is categorized as having a presenting distance visual acuity of less than 3/60 (20/400) in the better eye, or having a limitation of the field of vision to less than 10 degrees from the center of fixation. When defining visual impairment, three critical aspects of vision are considered: visual acuity, field of vision, and visual functioning.

Visual defects can result in the loss of clear vision, affecting either central or peripheral vision. These losses are measured through visual acuity, field of vision, and the level of visual functioning. Visual acuity refers to the eye's ability to see details. Distance visual acuity is measured as the maximum distance at which a person can see a specific object, divided by the maximum distance at which a person with normal eyesight can see the same object. The field of vision encompasses the area visible to the eyes when looking straight ahead. A simple method to test vision in children involves bringing a snapping finger from the side of the ear to the front, moving it up and down, and noting the position where the child first sees the finger. Visual functioning pertains to a person's ability to use their vision in daily activities.

The International Classification of Diseases categorizes vision impairment into two groups: distance and near presenting vision impairment.

Distance Vision Impairment Categories:

  - **Mild:** Visual acuity worse than 6/12 to 6/18

  - **Moderate:** Visual acuity worse than 6/18 to 6/60

  - **Severe:** Visual acuity worse than 6/60 to 3/60

  - **Blindness:** Visual acuity worse than 3/60

Near Vision Impairment Category:

  - Near visual acuity worse than N6 or M.08 at 40cm

These classifications help in understanding and addressing the varying degrees of visual impairment.

<u>**Diagnosis Of Visual Impairment/Blindness**</u>

An ophthalmologist or eye specialist diagnoses blindness in children by conducting a series of tests, assessing each eye individually. This is crucial as a child may experience sudden blindness in one or both eyes. The doctor will check the clarity of the child's vision and the extent of their visual range. One of the tests involves examining how the pupils react to light, checking if they dilate appropriately when exposed to direct light. Additionally, the doctor will assess the functioning of the eye muscles.

Visual impairment in newborns can often be detected from birth up to the age of 1 to 2 months. The causes of visual disabilities in children vary significantly across different countries. In low-income countries, congenital cataract is a leading cause of blindness, while in high-income countries, retinopathy of prematurity is more common. Globally, the leading causes of vision impairment include uncorrected refractive errors, cataract, glaucoma, diabetic retinopathy, and trachoma.

In cases where children have residual vision, assessing functional vision is critical. Functional vision assessment helps in understanding how children use their vision in daily activities and is essential for planning appropriate interventions and support.

Prevention of Blindness

Regular eye check-ups are crucial in preventing blindness. Periodic eye examinations ensure that any eye conditions are diagnosed early, allowing for timely intervention and treatment, which can prevent vision loss. Adhering to an ophthalmologist's instructions regarding care and medication for diagnosed eye diseases or infections is vital. If an individual experiences any signs of vision loss or suspects blindness, it is imperative to visit an ophthalmologist immediately for prompt treatment and potential recovery.

Parents should ensure their children's eyes are examined at key developmental stages. It is recommended to have their eyes checked at 6 months old, again at 3 years old, and then annually after they turn 6 years old. These regular check-ups are important to maintain eye health and prevent any onset of blindness. However, children born with blindness or with damage to the optic nerve of the eye will require specific treatments tailored to their condition.

Home Remedial Plan

ORIENTATION AND MOBILITY TECHNIQUES

When a person becomes blind, one of the primary challenges that arises is the ability to move independently and safely. It's often observed that visually impaired children experience delays in early motor development. Activities such as crawling, standing, sitting, and walking are typically delayed in these children. Therefore, it's crucial to develop orientation and mobility skills from the first year of their life. Orientation involves understanding the environment in which a visually impaired child lives. Due to distorted or absent visual inputs, these children must be trained in various skills that enable them to gather information through other senses — such as hearing, touch, smell, or kinesthetic awareness.

Mobility refers to the ability to physically move, involving changes in spatial location accomplished independently and in an upright position. This includes movements ranging from navigating within a single room to traveling between different locations or even countries. The capacity to move within and interact with the environment is critical, as it affects the individual's psychological, social, emotional, economic, and physical well-being. Restricted movement can significantly influence a child's development, understanding of concepts, and overall quality of life.

To enhance mobility and orientation, there are several techniques parents can use. These include the sighted guide technique, allowing the child to walk alone, or using a mobility device such as a cane. A cane typically extends from the floor to the user's waist and offers limited potential for independent movement. Training in mobility and orientation enables children to have a variety of real-life experiences, enhancing their understanding of concepts and interactions with their environment. Ultimately, mobility allows a child to perform daily activities independently, interact with others, and develop interpersonal relationships.

BRAILLE SYSTEM

Braille is a tactile reading and writing system, designed specifically for the visually impaired. The fundamental elements of Braille are known as Braille cells, which consist of six dots arranged in a rectangle. This arrangement is three dots high and two dots wide, or two columns and three rows. One of Braille's unique features is its basis in phonetics. In Braille, there are no distinct symbols for capital letters; instead, the first ten letters of the alphabet are repurposed to represent numbers.

There is a growing demand for a wide variety of materials to be available in Braille. To meet this need, several software programs have been developed for Braille translation, such as Duxbury MegaDots and Braille 2000. Additionally, scanning tools like OpenBook and Expert Reader enable users to scan and read a page in less than a minute.

Visually impaired children also have access to speech through various tools, including talking word processors, speech synthesizers, and screen-reading software. These tools enable students to hear letters, words, sentences, and phrases as they are inputted into the computer. Over the years, numerous Braille presses have been established in different regions to cater to the needs of the visually impaired. For example, the printing press in Dehradun has published a vast array of books for children with visual impairments.

HEARING IMPAIRMENT

Hearing impairment is a condition that can arise from structural abnormalities, such as a hole in the eardrum, and may lead to functional disability. However, according to the World Health Organization, being hearing impaired does not necessarily equate to being hearing handicapped. There are three main categories of hearing impairments:

1. Hearing Loss: This condition is present in individuals who cannot hear as well as someone with normal hearing. Normal hearing is characterized by a hearing threshold of 20 dB or better in both ears. Hearing loss can range from mild, moderate, severe, to profound and may affect one or both ears. This impairment can lead to difficulties in hearing conversational speech or loud sounds.

2. Hard of Hearing: This term refers to individuals with hearing loss that ranges from mild to severe. People who are hard of hearing usually communicate through spoken language and can benefit from hearing aids, cochlear implants, and other assistive devices.

3. Deaf: Individuals who are deaf typically have profound hearing loss, which means very little or no hearing capability. They often use sign language as their primary mode of communication. The impact of hearing loss can be more devastating when it occurs early in childhood, as it inhibits the child's ability to perceive everyday sounds like the chirping of birds, rustling of leaves, or distant voices. This can affect overall quality of life, leading to frustration, withdrawal from social activities, depression, and poor academic performance. Even mild hearing loss at an early age can result in significant challenges, including poor attention and academic difficulties. Therefore, early intervention and support are crucial.

Diagnosis Of Hearing Impairment

To diagnose hearing impairment, a thorough physical examination by a doctor is necessary. The doctor will examine the ears for any potential causes of hearing impairment, such as wax buildup or inflammation resulting from an infection. They will also look for any structural changes that could be contributing to hearing issues.

One common method for assessing hearing is for the doctor to whisper words while the patient covers one ear at a time. This test evaluates how well the patient can hear words spoken at different volumes and how they respond to the sounds. Additionally, a tuning fork test may be conducted. Tuning forks are two-pronged metal instruments that produce sound when struck. Simple tests using these forks can help the doctor detect significant hearing impairments and may also reveal where in the ear damage or infection has occurred.

It's important to note that children who are exposed to loud noises, including loud music, are at risk for hearing loss. Parents should seek medical attention immediately if their child experiences an ear infection, as untreated infections can cause permanent damage to the ear.

Treatment of Hearing Loss

If a child has severe hearing impairment and typical hearing aids are ineffective, a cochlear implant may be considered as an option. A cochlear implant works by bypassing damaged or non-functioning parts of the inner ear, directly stimulating the hearing nerve. The decision to use a cochlear implant typically involves consultation between an audiologist and an otolaryngologist (a medical doctor specializing in disorders of the ear, nose, and throat). They will discuss the potential benefits of a cochlear implant with the parents.

In some cases, hearing impairment can be caused by something as simple as ear wax blockage. A doctor can remove the wax using suction or other tools. Additionally, certain types of hearing impairments may be treated with surgery on the eardrum or the bones involved in hearing. If the hearing impairment is caused by damage to these structures, surgical intervention can be beneficial.

Home Remedial Plan

SPECIAL EDUCATION NEEDS

Children with hearing impairment often face difficulties in maintaining relationships with friends and family due to their inability to hear properly. While some can hear partially with the aid of hearing devices, they require extensive training to use these aids effectively. Many children with hearing impairments may also experience delayed speech and rely on sign language for communication.

Training in various areas is crucial for these children. Sign language is essential for those with complete hearing loss, while auditory verbal training benefits those with partial hearing loss. Parents can play a key role in teaching their children at home, helping to improve speech and develop total communication skills. This training might involve creating or dramatizing emotional concepts to handle different situations.

Additionally, parents can advocate for their child's needs in school settings. Requesting teachers to seat the child in the front row can facilitate better understanding and engagement in the classroom. Collaborating with teachers and school staff to provide clear, face-to-face instructions can also aid in lip-reading. Utilizing visual aids like transparencies, chalkboards, flashcards, etc., can enhance learning. Providing written handouts of classroom instructions is another effective strategy to support these children's educational needs.

CEREBRAL PALSY

Cerebral palsy is a congenital disorder resulting from abnormal brain development or damage to the developing brain. This condition primarily affects a person's ability to move, maintain balance, and posture. The term 'cerebral' refers to the brain, while 'palsy' indicates weakness or problems with muscle use. The symptoms of cerebral palsy vary widely among individuals.

A child with mild cerebral palsy may experience slight awkwardness in walking or difficulty in maintaining good posture but can typically perform daily tasks independently. In contrast, a child with severe cerebral palsy may require special equipment to walk, or in some cases, may not be able to walk at all. Children with severe cerebral palsy may also be wheelchair-bound, especially if all limbs are affected.

While some children with cerebral palsy may only have movement and postural difficulties, others may experience associated conditions. These can include intellectual disabilities, visual and hearing impairments, and speech deficits. Each case of cerebral palsy is unique, and the level of support and intervention required varies based on the severity and associated conditions.

The most prevalent form of cerebral palsy is spastic cerebral palsy, accounting for about 80% of cerebral palsy cases. In spastic CP, the muscles are stiff, making movements awkward. This condition is further divided into three types, each affecting different limbs of the body:

1. **Diplegia:** In diplegic cerebral palsy, muscle stiffness primarily affects the legs, while the arms are less affected or not affected at all. Children with diplegia may have difficulty walking due to tight hip and leg muscles.

2. **Hemiplegia:** This type of cerebral palsy affects only one side of the child's body. Typically, the upper limb or arm is more affected than the leg.

3. **Quadriplegia:** Quadriplegic cerebral palsy is the most severe form, involving all four limbs. Often, facial muscles are also impacted, leading to challenges such as poor facial muscle control and excessive drooling. Children with spastic quadriplegia are usually unable to walk and often have associated developmental disabilities, including intellectual disability, vision and hearing impairments, and speech deficits.

Diagnosis Of Cerebral Palsy

The early signs of cerebral palsy can vary significantly due to the diverse types of disabilities and conditions that may be associated with it. A primary indicator that a child might have cerebral palsy is a delay in reaching motor milestones. This delay includes missing movement milestones such as rolling over, sitting with or without support, standing with or without support, or walking. It's important to note that some children without cerebral palsy might also exhibit some of these signs due to abnormal brain development or other associated conditions.

For parents assessing a baby younger than 6 months of age, look for these signs:

- The child's head lags when you pick them up while they are lying on their back.

- The child feels stiff and exhibits limited movement.

- When held in the arms, the child seems to overextend their back and neck, appearing to push away from you.

- The child's legs become stiff and cross in a scissor-like manner when you pick them up.

- The child reaches out with only one hand while keeping the other hand fisted.

- The child scoots on their buttocks or hops on their knees but does not crawl on all fours.

Identifying these early signs can be crucial for timely intervention and management of cerebral palsy.

Treatment and Therapies

Although there is no cure for cerebral palsy, a congenital disorder, various treatments and therapies can significantly improve the life of a child with CP, helping them to become an integral part of society. It's crucial to start treatment programs as early as possible. Once a CP diagnosis is confirmed, parents should work with a physiotherapist to develop both short-term and long-term goals to help the child reach their full potential. Common treatments for children with severe CP include medications, surgery, braces, and physiotherapy.

Early intervention is particularly important for children with CP, as it aids in their development and preparation for school. Both early intervention and school-aged services are available through special education programs and the Individuals with Disabilities Education Act (IDEA). The brain abnormalities or damage leading to CP can occur before birth, during birth, within a month after birth, or during the first year of life while the brain is still developing. However, 85% to 90% of CP cases are congenital, meaning they occur before birth.

If parents suspect that their child is not meeting developmental milestones or may have CP, they should contact their healthcare provider immediately. Many states offer free evaluation programs to diagnose CP. For children with mild or moderate CP, parents can encourage at least 40 minutes of physical exercise five days a week. For toddlers or young children, body massages can help reduce muscle stiffness.

Each child with CP is unique, with varying needs and challenges. Parents should tailor routine exercises and educational activities to maximize benefits for their child. Dancing is an excellent activity for practicing coordination and moving multiple body parts simultaneously. Swimming is also beneficial, as it can aid in walking and strengthening muscles. Additionally, outdoor play, such as going to the park, is a natural way to encourage activity and address sensory issues.

DOWN SYNDROME

Down syndrome is a genetic disorder that leads to developmental and intellectual delays in children. To understand Down syndrome, it's essential to know about chromosomes, which are small packages of genes in the body. Typically, a child is born with 46 chromosomes, but children with Down syndrome have an extra copy of one of these chromosomes, specifically chromosome 21. This condition, medically termed trisomy, means Down syndrome is also referred to as Trisomy 21. This additional genetic material alters the development of the baby's body and brain, resulting in both mental challenges, such as intellectual disability, and physical challenges.

Children with Down syndrome often exhibit distinctive physical features. These can include a flattened facial profile, a depressed nasal bridge, a short neck, small ears, poor muscle tone, loose joints, small hands and feet, and a shorter stature.

A major risk factor for having a child with Down syndrome is the age of the mother. Women who are 35 years or older when they become pregnant have a higher likelihood of having a child with Down syndrome compared to younger women. Interestingly, the majority of babies with Down syndrome are born to mothers over 30 years old. While many children with Down syndrome have common facial features and no other significant birth defects, some individuals with the condition may have one or more major birth defects, such as heart or thyroid problems, in addition to intellectual disability.

Diagnosis of Down Syndrome

With advancements in medical science, there are two primary types of tests available for detecting Down syndrome during pregnancy: screening tests and diagnostic tests.

Screening tests typically involve a combination of blood tests that measure various substances in the mother's blood. Additionally, an ultrasound is often used to examine the developing baby in the womb. During the ultrasound, one of the key indicators technicians look for is the thickness of fluid behind the baby's neck, as excess fluid in this area can be indicative of a genetic anomaly. These screening tests help assess the baby's risk of having Down syndrome.

If the results of the screening tests raise concerns or if there's a need for more definitive information, diagnostic tests can be performed. These tests are designed to confirm the presence of Down syndrome. The types of diagnostic tests include:

1. Amniocentesis: This procedure involves examining the amniotic fluid surrounding the fetus.

2. Chorionic Villus Sampling (CVS): CVS involves taking a sample of the placental tissue.

3. Percutaneous Umbilical Blood Sampling (PUBS): In PUBS, blood is taken from the umbilical cord for examination.

These diagnostic tests provide more definitive information regarding the risk or presence of Down syndrome in the fetus.

Home Remedial Plan

TREATMENT OF DOWN SYNDROME

Down syndrome is a lifelong condition, and while there is no specific cure, various therapies can significantly improve a child's physical and intellectual abilities. Children with Down syndrome often thrive with routine and respond more positively to support rather than discipline. Parents can aid their development by creating and adhering to a daily schedule. Transitioning between activities should be facilitated with clear signals. Visual aids, like picture schedules, can be used to outline daily tasks and placed in a visible area for the child.

Instructions should be simplified and tasks broken down into smaller steps. Use clear, simple language and limit instructions to one or two steps at a time. Creating a safe play area in the home allows the child to play independently. It's also beneficial for a parent to regularly engage in activities such as playing, reading, and going on outings with the child. Encouraging the child to give directions to familiar places, like the barber shop or grocery store, can enhance their orientation skills.

In academics, support from parents, teachers, and school staff is crucial. Breaking down instructions and helping the child understand school lessons can be very effective. Parents should look for ways to reinforce what the child is learning at school at home. Children with mild to moderate levels of Down syndrome can integrate well into society and the community. Education, up to a certain level, is achievable, and functional academics can be a focus. Training in daily routine tasks and life skills is essential.

With appropriate training and therapies, children with Down syndrome can take on job responsibilities, helping them to become more independent. This support not only enhances their skills but also fosters a sense of belonging and contribution to society.

EARLY INTERVENTION PROGRAMS

Early intervention is crucial when raising a child with disabilities. It involves planning and organizing activities that foster a child's development across various domains, including language, cognitive, behavioral, social, and emotional aspects. Parents should design activities based on their child's current abilities and developmental needs. While some early intervention activities, particularly therapeutic ones, require professional involvement, many can be learned and carried out by parents at home.

Research underscores the significance of the first six years in a child's life as a critical period for development in all areas. During this time, the brain exhibits greater plasticity, meaning children with disabilities can benefit substantially from various therapies. This period is characterized by the most rapid rate of learning and development for these children. Since language development often occurs incidentally, there are considerable opportunities for children to acquire speech and language skills quickly in a home environment.

To enhance communication, parents should engage in constant dialogue with their child. This can involve singing to the child and using gestures to encourage imitation of sounds and actions. Incorporating speech and language development into everyday activities is beneficial. Oral stimulation exercises, such as using a straw for drinking, blowing balloons or whistles, and brushing the inside of the mouth, can also be helpful.

Playing games with flashcards depicting fruits and vegetables, where the child is asked to name the pictured items, can be an engaging way to develop recognition and speech. Additionally, seeking professional help for home-based intervention programs can provide parents with further training in early intervention, as well as valuable supervision and guidance.

Advantages of Home Remedial Plan

Children with disabilities often learn best in their natural environment, with training provided either by professionals or by parents. Active parental involvement in the child's learning process is crucial and convenient, as it eliminates the need for transport arrangements and the expenses of professional training. While professional assistance is undoubtedly beneficial, many effective stimulation materials are readily available at home and are simple to use.

A practical approach is for parents to initially engage a professional trainer or therapist for in-home sessions. This enables all family members to learn intervention activities and apply them with the child. Such an approach ensures the child receives ample stimulation and interaction opportunities, while also allowing the parents to share responsibilities.

However, due to financial constraints, professional therapists may only be able to make a limited number of visits to some households. In such cases, it's highly recommended for parents to learn the techniques themselves. This not only helps in coping with the child's disability but also in managing behavior issues as the child grows. A positive parenting approach and creating a happy, playful environment can effectively address behavior challenges.

If parents encounter significant behavior issues over a short period, a center-based early intervention program may be advisable. In such programs, a pediatrician often supervises, with professional therapists and experienced special educators providing a structured system of training. Parents can mirror these techniques at home, maintaining routine and consistency, and periodically visit the center for further guidance and support.

SPECIFIC LEARNING DISABILITIES

Specific learning disabilities refer to a diverse group of conditions characterized by deficits in processing language, whether spoken or written. This can manifest as difficulties in understanding, speaking, reading, writing, spelling, or performing mathematical calculations. Such disabilities encompass a range of conditions, including perceptual disabilities, dyslexia, dysgraphia, dyspraxia, and developmental aphasia.

The Individuals with Disabilities Education Act (IDEA) defines a specific learning disability as a disorder in one or more basic psychological processes involved in understanding or using spoken or written language. This may result in challenges with listening, thinking, speaking, reading, writing, spelling, or mathematical calculations. The definition includes conditions such as perceptual disabilities, brain injury, minimal brain dysfunction, dyslexia, and developmental aphasia. It is noted, however, that this term does not encompass learning problems primarily resulting from visual, hearing, or motor disabilities.

Learning disabilities often stem from genetic factors influencing brain function, impacting one or more cognitive processes related to learning. These processing issues can hinder the acquisition of basic skills like reading, writing, and math, and also affect higher-level skills, including organization, time management, abstract reasoning, memory, and attention.

It's crucial to recognize that learning disabilities can impact aspects of life beyond academia, influencing relationships with family, friends, and within the workplace. While difficulties with reading, writing, and math are often identified during school years, leading to diagnosis, some individuals might not be evaluated until they reach higher education or enter the workforce. Others may never receive a formal evaluation, living their lives without understanding the reasons behind their academic and interpersonal challenges.

Identification and Assessment of Specific Learning Disability

A study by the National Institute of Mental Health (NIMH) found that 67% of young students at risk for reading difficulties became average readers after receiving early intervention. Teachers and parents are often the first to notice signs of a learning disability in a child. Diagnosing a learning disability can be complex, so it's crucial not to jump to conclusions about your child's challenges without professional advice. Always consult a professional, such as a registered psychologist, for a proper evaluation.

Intervention is essential, regardless of whether the child's difficulties stem from a learning disability. The process of diagnosing a learning disability typically involves testing, history-taking, and observation by trained special educators and psychologists. Often, a team of professionals coordinates to obtain an accurate diagnosis.

<u>To help parents identify if their child might have an SLD, here are some key characteristics to look out for:</u>

- Difficulty maintaining attention while performing tasks.

- Challenges in completing tasks within given time limits.

- A pattern of consistent errors, such as omitting letters while reading.

- Difficulty copying from the blackboard without missing letters or words.

- Problems associating sounds with the alphabet.

- Difficulty in understanding or explaining concepts in subjects like science or social studies.

- Struggles with comprehending word problems and understanding their meaning and relationships.

- Difficulty differentiating similar letters (e.g., B and D) or numbers (e.g., 9 and 6).

Recognizing these signs can be the first step in seeking the necessary help and interventions for a child with a specific learning disability.

<u>Assessment Tool for Specific Learning Disabilities (SLD)</u>

<u>Introduction: An overview of the assessment tool and its objectives.</u>

<u>VISUAL PERCEPTION:</u>

1.   Figure-Ground Perception: Ability to distinguish a figure from the background.

2.   Form Constancy Perception: Recognizing forms and objects regardless of their orientation, size, or position.

3. Visual Discrimination: Differentiating one object from another.

4. Visual Closure: Identifying incomplete figures when only fragments are presented.

5. Position in Space Perception: Understanding spatial relationships between objects.

6.   Visual Spatial Perception: Perceiving the spatial orientation of objects.

7. Visual Sequential Memory: Remembering the order of objects or images.

8. Visual Non-Sequential Memory: Recalling visual information without a specific order.

AUDITORY PERCEPTION:

1. Auditory Figure-Ground: Differentiating primary sounds from background noise.

2. Auditory Discrimination: Distinguishing between different sounds or words.

3. Auditory Blending: Combining individual sounds into words.

4. Auditory Analysis: Breaking down words into individual sounds.

5. Auditory Closure: Understanding incomplete words or sentences.

6. Auditory Sequential Memory: Remembering sequences of sounds or information.

7. Auditory Non-Sequential Memory: Recalling auditory information without a specific order.

LANGUAGE:

1. Receptive Language: Assessing listening and reading comprehension skills.

2. Expressive Language: Evaluating oral and written expression abilities.

Mathematical Skills: Evaluating basic mathematical understanding and abilities.

Graphomotor Skills: Assessing the ability to perform tasks requiring hand-eye coordination.

Logical and Abstract Reasoning Skills: Evaluating the ability to reason and solve problems.

Rubrics and Final Scoring: Guidelines for interpreting the assessment results and final scoring method.

This structured assessment tool is designed to evaluate various aspects critical to identifying specific learning disabilities, providing valuable insights for targeted interventions.

INTRODUCTION TO INFORMAL ASSESSMENTS

An informal assessment is a spontaneous, flexible testing method used to evaluate a participant's knowledge using age-appropriate subject tests and specifically designed rubrics. Special educators or parents conduct these assessments by asking open-ended questions and observing the child's performance, thereby gauging their understanding and skills. The assessments are content and performance-driven, tailored by a team of special educators to suit the specific needs and curriculum of classes 4 and 5.

The role of parents or special educators during these assessments is to encourage the child to produce, construct, demonstrate, or perform responses. These assessments are practical, focusing on material and activities that the child is currently engaged with in the classroom. They offer flexibility in administration and interpretation, such as allowing extra time, which can put the child at ease and encourage their best effort.

Informal assessments can be conducted more frequently than formal assessments and serve as valuable observational tools. They help in identifying a child's strengths and weaknesses, informing future lesson planning, and making immediate adjustments to the learning process. These methods are particularly useful in determining a child's need for independence or support in the classroom, including the potential use of a buddy system.

A key aspect of informal assessments is their ability to actively involve the child in the evaluation process. This involvement aids both parents and teachers in understanding the child's current level and in planning lessons accordingly. The assessment tool includes definitions of various concepts and worksheets at two levels: Level 1 and Level 2. The child is first given Level 1 worksheets, and if successful, they progress to Level 2. While this tool is not a formally approved testing system, it can be immensely helpful for parents to gauge their child's current level of functioning.

INFORMAL ASSESSMENT (VISUAL)

Visual Discrimination Assessment - Level 1

Visual Discrimination: This skill involves the ability to discern differences in, and classify, objects, symbols, or shapes. It encompasses categorization based on various attributes such as color, position, form, pattern, and size. Visual discrimination enables a child to notice subtle differences between objects or pictures and to determine if items match or are similar.

These rubrics are designed to evaluate a child's visual discrimination ability, which is crucial for their cognitive development and learning processes. Achieving a satisfactory score in Level 1 is necessary to progress to Level 2, ensuring the student is adequately equipped for more advanced challenges in visual discrimination.

Task: Circle the picture in each group that does not belong.

Instructions: Below are five groups of pictures. In each group, one picture is different from the others. Circle the picture that does not fit with the rest in each group. Each correct answer is worth 2 marks.

Scoring Criteria:

- Each question is worth 2 marks.

- Total marks for this task: 10

- Scoring 60% and above: Satisfactory performance, eligible to move to Level 2

- Scoring below 60%: Needs further practice and remediation

This task aims to evaluate the child's visual discrimination skills, specifically their ability to identify items that do not logically fit within a set. This skill is essential for cognitive development and learning processes.

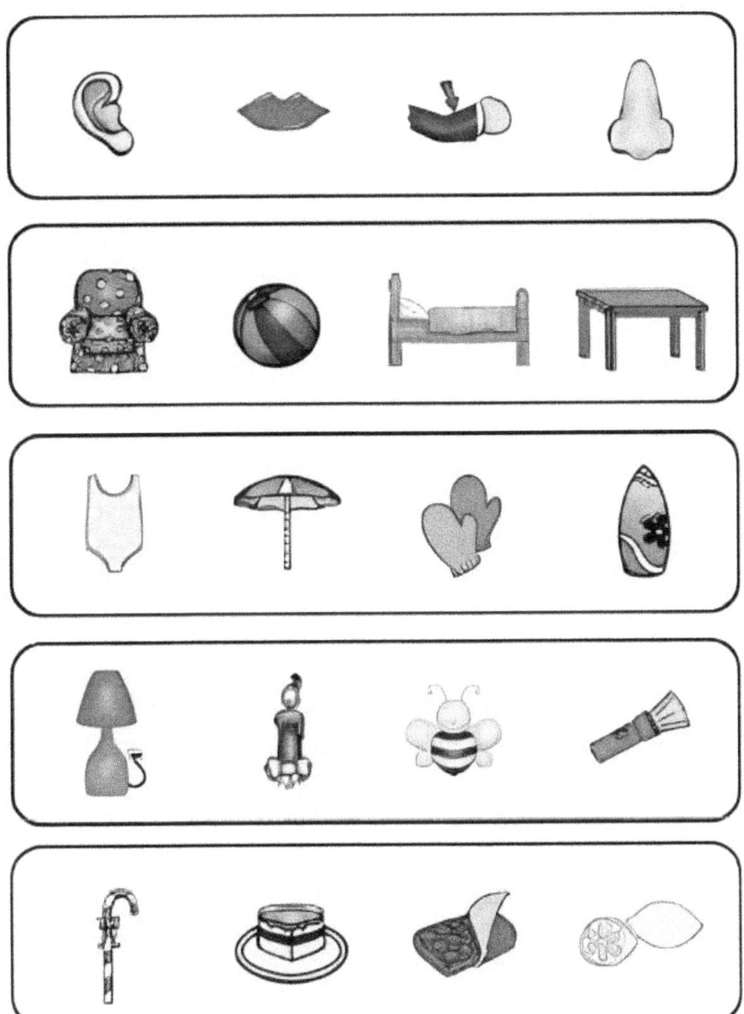

Visual Discrimination Assessment - Level 2

Task: Connect merged shapes to their corresponding individual shapes.

Instructions:

1. Teach the child five different shapes: circle, square, triangle, pentagon, and hexagon.

2. Present the child with a picture that has these shapes merged or overlapped in a complex design.

3. Provide individual pictures of each of the five shapes separately.

4. The child must identify and connect each shape from the complex design to its corresponding individual shape.

Scoring Criteria:

- 2 marks are awarded for each correctly identified and connected shape.

- Total marks for this task: 10 (5 shapes x 2 marks each)

- Scoring 60% and above: Satisfactory performance

- Scoring below 60%: Needs further practice and remediation

This task assesses the child's ability to discriminate between shapes within a complex visual arrangement, a skill that is crucial for visual processing and cognitive development. Success in this task indicates an enhanced level of visual discrimination capability.

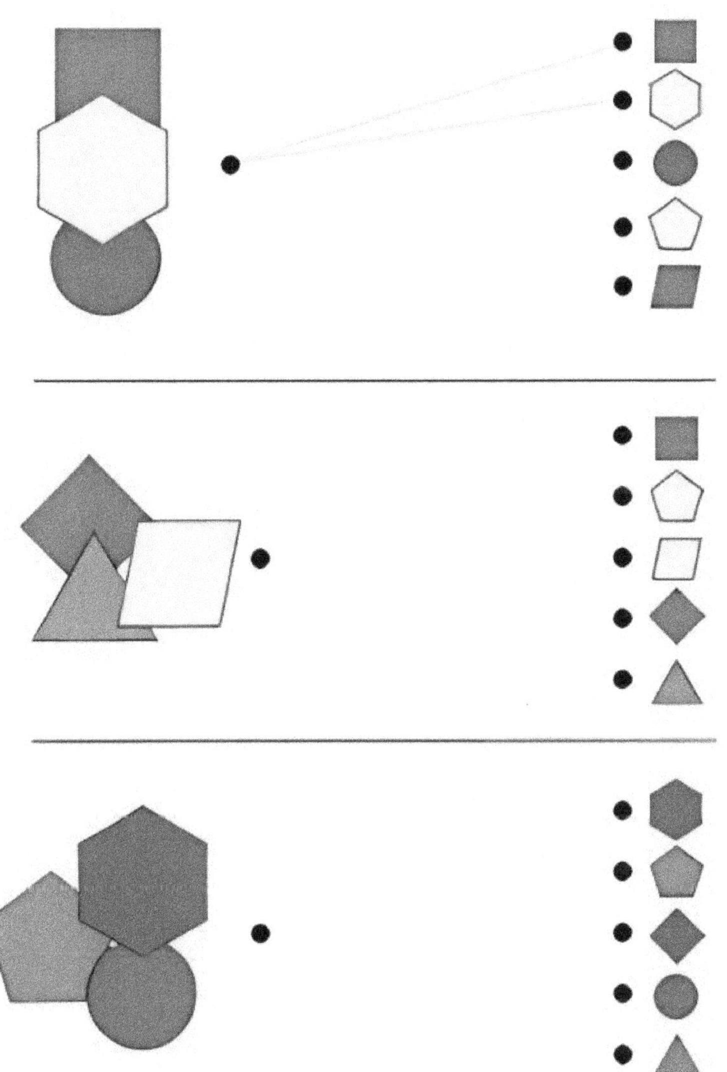

Visual Figure-Ground Perception Assessment - Level 1

Visual Figure-Ground Perception: This concept refers to the visual system's ability to simplify a scene into a primary object (the figure) that we focus on, and everything else that forms the background (the ground). This process involves distinguishing the main image (figure) from the background (ground).

These rubrics are designed to evaluate a child's ability to differentiate between the main object and the background in a visual scene. The progression to Level 2 depends on achieving a satisfactory performance in Level 1, ensuring that the child is ready for more advanced assessments in visual figure-ground perception.

Task: Identify the main object in each picture.

Instructions:

1. Present the child with a series of images, each containing a primary object set against a detailed background.

2. Ask the child to identify the main object in each image.

Scoring Criteria:

- Each correctly identified main object earns 2 marks.

- Total marks for this task: 12 (6 images x 2 marks each)

- Scoring 60% and above: Satisfactory performance, eligible to move to Level 2

- Scoring below 60%: Needs further practice and remediation

This assessment aims to evaluate the child's ability to focus on primary objects despite potentially distracting backgrounds, a key aspect of visual figure-ground perception. The task is designed to be engaging and appropriate for a Level 1 assessment.

Find the items!

Circle the images you can find from the list below:

Visual Figure-Ground Perception Assessment - Level 2

Task: Identify multiple objects or specific details in complex images.

Instructions:

1.   Present the child with a series of more complex and detailed images than in Level 1.

2.   In each image, there are multiple objects or specific details that the child must identify against intricate backgrounds.

3.   The child needs to distinguish and point out these objects or details.

Scoring Criteria:

- Each correctly identified object or detail in the image earns 2 marks.

- Total marks for this task: 12 (6 images with multiple objects/details to identify)

- Scoring 60% and above: Satisfactory performance, successful completion of Level 2

- Scoring below 60%: Needs further practice and remediation

This Level 2 assessment is designed to test and further develop the child's advanced visual figure-ground perception skills. Success in this task indicates a higher level of ability to process and interpret visual information in complex scenes.

Find the items!

How many of each can you find in the box below?

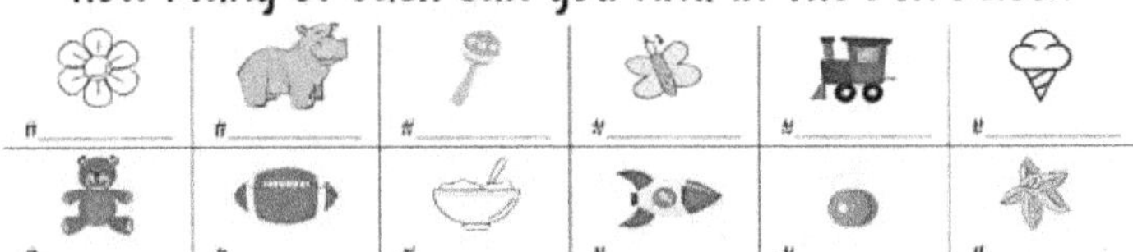

Visual Spatial Skills Assessment - Level 1

Visual-Spatial Perception: This skill involves recognizing an object's physical location and understanding the spatial relationships between objects. It encompasses a range of specific abilities within the visual domain, such as locating points in space, determining the orientation of lines and objects, assessing depth, appreciating geometric relations between objects, and processing motion, including motion in depth.

These rubrics are designed to assess a child's visual-spatial perception abilities. This skill is crucial for cognitive development and understanding the physical world. Achieving a satisfactory score in Level 1 is necessary to progress to Level 2, ensuring that the student is adequately prepared for more advanced challenges in visual-spatial perception.

Task: Match the word with the correct image of a cat.

Instructions:

1. Present the child with a series of words, each describing a specific type of cat.

2. Accompany these words with multiple images of cats, each differing in appearance based on the descriptive word.

3. The child must identify and mark the image of the cat that matches each descriptive word.

Scoring Criteria:

- Each correctly matched word-image pair earns 2 marks.

- Total marks for this task: 10 (5 matches x 2 marks each)

- Scoring 60% and above: Satisfactory performance, eligible to move to Level 2

- Scoring below 60%: Needs further practice and remediation

This assessment aims to evaluate the child's basic visual spatial skills, specifically their ability to match descriptive words with corresponding visual images. It is an engaging way to assess how well a child can correlate verbal descriptions with visual characteristics.

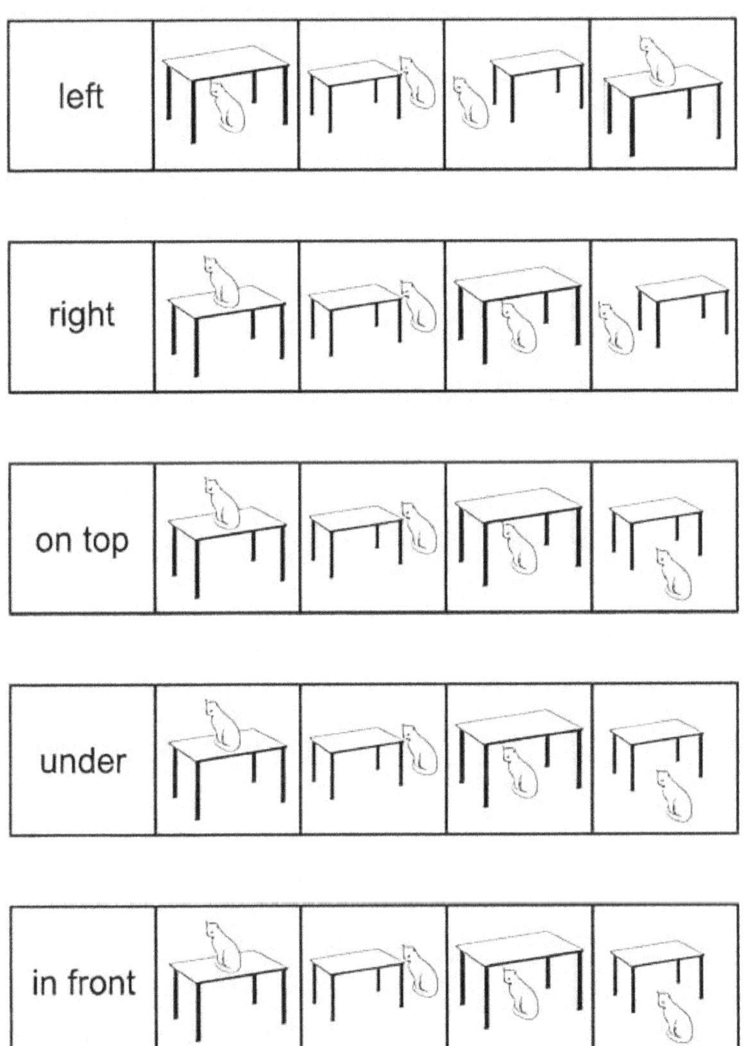
left
right
on top
under
in front

Visual Spatial Skills Assessment - Level 2

Task: Match the word with the correct image of a circle.

Instructions:

1. Present the child with a series of words, each describing a specific attribute or feature of a circle.

2. Accompany these words with multiple images of circles, each differing based on the descriptive word.

3. The child must identify and mark the image of the circle that matches each descriptive word.

Scoring Criteria:

- Each correctly matched word-image pair earns 2 marks.

- Total marks for this task: 10 (5 matches x 2 marks each)

- Scoring 60% and above: Satisfactory performance, successful completion of Level 2

- Scoring below 60%: Needs further practice and remediation

This Level 2 assessment is designed to test and further develop the child's advanced visual spatial skills, particularly their ability to associate verbal descriptions with visual patterns and features. Success in this task indicates a higher level of ability to process and interpret complex visual information.

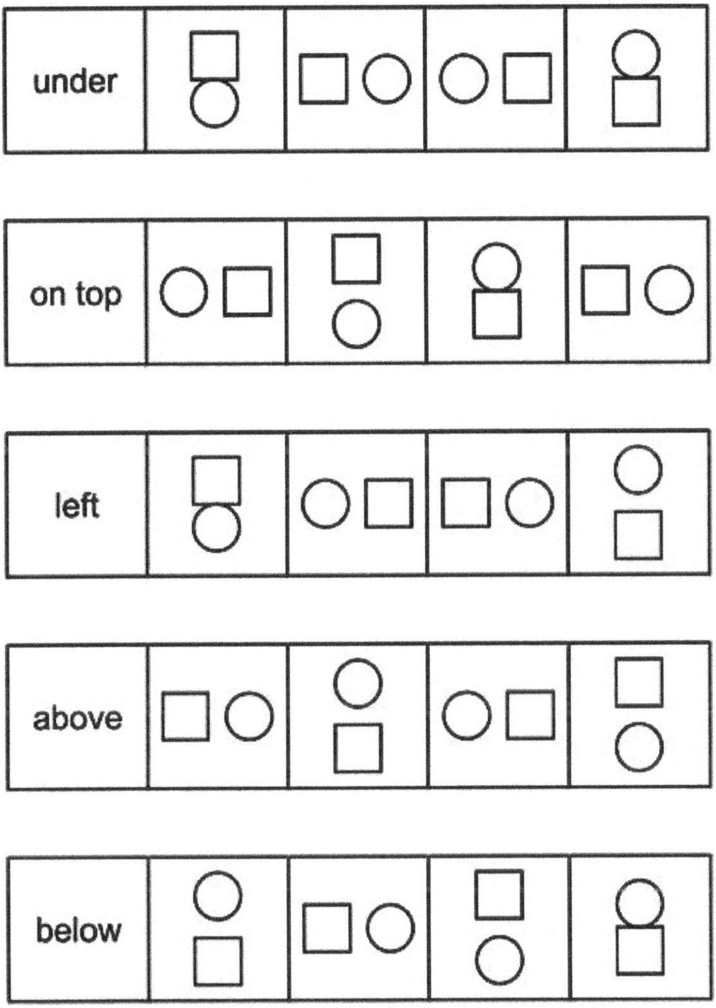

under				
on top				
left				
above				
below				

Visual Form Constancy Assessment - Level 1

Form Constancy: This visual perception skill enables an individual to recognize and label objects even when they are viewed from different angles or in various environments. It helps students understand that the form, shape, or object remains constant despite changes in size, position, or context.

These rubrics aim to evaluate a student's ability to maintain object constancy across different perspectives and settings. Achieving a satisfactory score in Level 1 is necessary to progress to Level 2, ensuring that the student is adequately prepared for more advanced challenges in form constancy.

Task: Color the arrows based on their direction.

Instructions:

1. Present the child with four arrows, each pointing in a different direction (up, down, left, right) and colored in a specific color.

2. Provide a series of uncolored arrows, each pointing in one of the four directions.

3.   The child must color these arrows according to the direction they point, matching the color of the example arrows.

Scoring Criteria:

- Each correctly colored arrow earns 2 marks.

- Total marks for this task: 8 [the number of arrows x 2 marks each (depending on the total number of arrows provided)]

- Scoring 60% and above: Satisfactory performance, eligible to move to Level 2

- Scoring below 60%:   Needs further practice and remediation

This assessment aims to evaluate the child's visual form constancy skills, particularly their ability to recognize and apply consistent characteristics (color) based on the form's orientation (direction of the arrow). It is an engaging way to assess how well a child can maintain consistency in visual recognition and application.

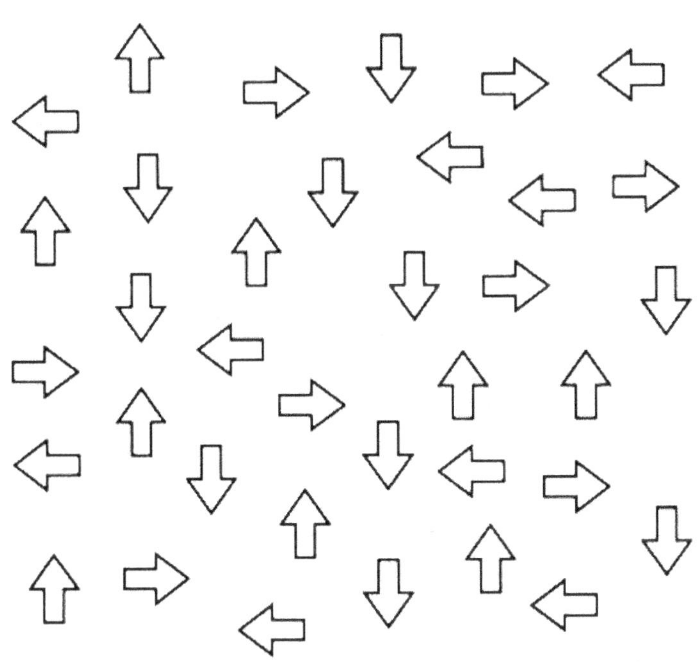

Visual Form Constancy Assessment - Level 2

Task: Identify and circle the letter in each row that matches the first letter.

Instructions:

1. Present the child with several rows of letters. Each row begins with a specific letter, followed by a series of different letters.

2. The child's task is to circle the letter in each row that matches the first letter of that row.

Scoring Criteria:

- Each correctly circled matching letter earns 2 marks.

- Total marks for this task: 10 (5 rows x 2 marks each)

- Scoring 60% and above: Satisfactory performance, successful completion of Level 2

- Scoring below 60%: Needs further practice and remediation

This assessment tests the child's visual form constancy skills at a more advanced level, focusing on their ability to recognize and consistently identify the same letter among a variety of others. Success in this task indicates a developed skill in maintaining visual constancy amidst varying visual stimuli.

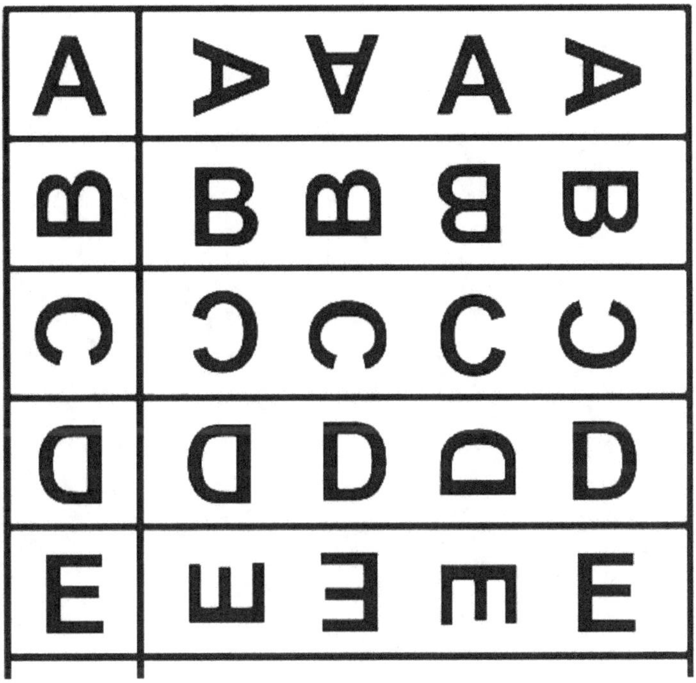

Visual Closure Assessment - Level 1

Visual Closure: This skill refers to the brain's ability to recognize a familiar item, word, or picture when only a small part of it is visible. It involves the mind using past information to 'fill in the blanks' and visualize the whole. Visual closure enables the correct perception of an object or word, even when it is partially obscured or incomplete.

These rubrics are designed to assess a child's proficiency in visual closure. The ability to interpret partially visible objects or words is critical for cognitive development and learning. Achieving a satisfactory score in Level 1 is necessary for advancement to Level 2, ensuring the student is ready for more complex challenges in visual closure.

Task: Identify the complete form of partially displayed numbers.

Instructions:

1. Present the child with a series of examples, each showing a number with a missing part.

2. Provide a list of complete numbers next to each example.

3. The child's task is to identify which complete number corresponds to the incomplete one in each example.

Scoring Criteria:

- Each correctly identified complete number earns 2 marks.

- Total marks for this task: 10 (5 examples x 2 marks each)

- Scoring 60% and above: Satisfactory performance, eligible to move to Level 2

- Scoring below 60%: Needs further practice and remediation

This assessment aims to evaluate the child's visual closure skills, particularly their ability to perceive and mentally complete partially displayed numbers. It's a fundamental skill for visual processing and understanding incomplete visual information.

2	৭	५	੭
3	৬	৩	৪
5	५	੨	৬
6	੭	੮	৪
9	৪	৬	५

Visual Closure Assessment - Level 2

Task: Complete the incomplete shapes.

Instructions:

1. Present the child with eight shapes, each only partially drawn.

2. The child's task is to complete these shapes by drawing in the missing parts.

Scoring Criteria:

- Each correctly completed shape earns 1 mark.

- Total marks for this task: 8 (1 mark per shape)

- Scoring 60% and above: Satisfactory performance, successful completion of Level 2

- Scoring below 60%: Needs further practice and remediation

This Level 2 assessment is designed to test and develop the child's advanced visual closure skills, focusing on their ability to perceive and complete partially drawn shapes. This task not only assesses visual recognition but also the child's ability to engage in spatial reasoning and fine motor control. Success in this task indicates a developed capacity to interpret and interact with incomplete visual information.

Rectangle	Triangle
Star	Circle
Square	Oval
Diamond	Heart

Visual Sequential Memory Assessment - Level 1

Visual Sequential Memory: This ability involves remembering and recalling a sequence of objects or events in their correct order. It is a critical skill for various academic tasks, including reading, spelling, reading comprehension, math, and the ability to copy information from the board to a notebook.

These rubrics are designed to assess a child's visual sequential memory. This skill is crucial for learning and executing tasks that require the ability to follow sequences. Achieving a satisfactory score in Level 1 is necessary to progress to Level 2, ensuring that the student is ready for more complex challenges in visual sequential memory.

Task: Remember and replicate the order of given designs.

Instructions:

1. Present the child with a series of simple designs arranged in a specific order.

2. Allow the child some time to observe and memorize the sequence of these designs.

3. Cover the original designs and provide the child with blank spaces (blocks or sections on a paper) to replicate the designs in the correct order from memory.

Scoring Criteria:

- Each correctly replicated design in the correct sequence earns 2 marks.

- Total marks for this task: 10 (5 designs x 2 marks each)

- Scoring 60% and above: Satisfactory performance, eligible to move to Level 2

- Scoring below 60%: Needs further practice and remediation

This Level 1 assessment aims to evaluate the child's basic visual sequential memory skills. It tests their ability to remember and replicate a sequence of visual information, a fundamental skill for learning and cognitive development. This task also helps in assessing the child's attention to detail and short-term memory capacity.

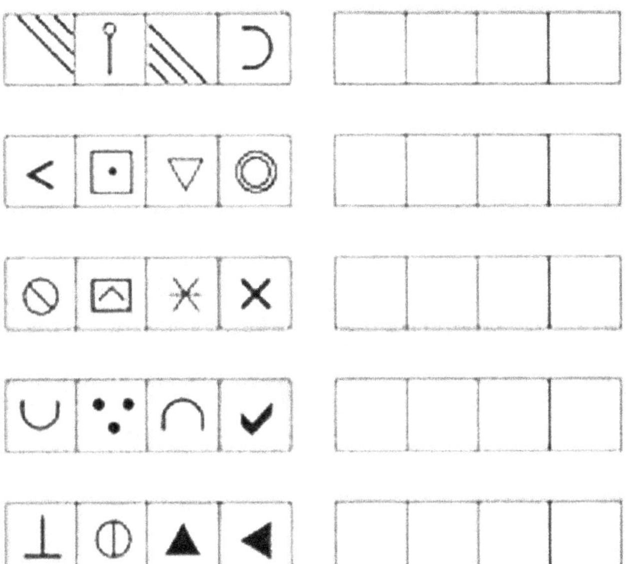

Visual Sequential Memory Assessment - Level 2

Task: Number the sequence of events in a story.

Instructions:

1. Present the child with a story divided into several key events or images, each depicting a different part of the narrative. The story should be about a baker baking cookies for kids, with each event/image representing a step in this process.

2. The events/images are initially presented out of order.

3. The child's task is to write numbers next to each event/image to place them in the correct sequence, as they would logically occur in the story.

Scoring Criteria:

- Each event correctly sequenced earns 2 marks.

- Total marks for this task: 10 (assuming 5 events/images)

- Scoring 60% and above: Satisfactory performance, successful completion of Level 2

- Scoring below 60%: Needs further practice and remediation

This Level 2 assessment is designed to test the child's advanced visual sequential memory skills, focusing on their ability to understand and arrange a sequence of events logically. This task not only assesses memory but also the child's comprehension of logical processes and storytelling.

A baker is mixing
the cookie batter.

The cookies are
ready.

He placed the tray
into the oven.

Kids are eating the
cookies.

He is filling the mould
with the batter.

INFORMAL ASSESSMENT (AUDITORY)

Auditory Figure-Ground Perception Assessment - Level 1

Auditory Figure-Ground Perception: This skill enables an individual to focus on specific sounds amidst a background of different noises. It's essential for scenarios such as a child listening to a teacher's voice in a noisy classroom.

These rubrics are designed to measure a child's ability to distinguish primary sounds from surrounding noise. Achieving a satisfactory score on Level 1 indicates readiness for more advanced auditory perception challenges in Level 2. Regular assessment and remediation can strengthen this vital auditory skill, enhancing the child's ability to focus in environments with competing sounds.

Task: Listening Comprehension

Instructions:

1. Read a short passage aloud to the child. The passage should be clear and appropriate for the child's age and comprehension level.

2.   After reading the passage, ask the child a series of questions based on what was read.

3.   The child's task is to answer these questions, demonstrating their ability to focus on and comprehend the auditory information provided.

Scoring Criteria:

- Each correctly answered question earns 2 marks.

- Total marks for this task: 10 (5 questions x 2 marks each)

- Scoring 60% and above: Satisfactory performance, eligible to move to Level 2

- Scoring below 60%: Needs further practice and remediation

This Level 1 assessment is designed to evaluate the child's ability to concentrate on spoken words and comprehend their content, despite potential auditory distractions. It tests listening skills and the ability to extract key information from a narrative, fundamental aspects of auditory figure-ground perception.

HAPPY BIRTHDAY

Maryam is having a birthday party. Her birthday is March 14th. She is turning eight years old. Maryam invited all her friends from school to her birthday party. Nine friends from school came to her party. Her Grandma and Grandpa also came. Maryam's Mom served chocolate cake and vanilla ice cream. There was also pizza and juice to drink. The kids played games at the party. There were a lot of balloons at the birthday party. The girls tried to pop most of them. Maryam blew out the candles on her birthday cake, then she opened her presents. She got lots of dolls and toys from her friends. Her grandparents got her a pretty new dress.

Read the above passage and do the following activities.

1. Choose the best option.

1. Maryam's birthday is on   14 August / 14 March / 14 April

2. How old is Maryam?   6 years / 7 years / 8 years

3. Her grandparents got her a   doll / toys / dress

2. Fill in the blanks.

(i)   Maryam invited all her friends from ________________.

(ii)   ________________ friends from school came to her party.

(iii)   Maryam's mom served chocolate cake and ________________ ice cream.

(iv)   There was ________________ to drink.

Auditory Figure-Ground Perception Assessment - Level 2

Task: Advanced Listening Comprehension

Instructions:

1. Read a passage aloud to the child that is more complex and detailed compared to Level 1. The passage should be suitable for the child's age but should include more characters, events, or descriptive information.

2. After reading the passage, ask the child a series of more detailed and inferential questions based on the content.

3. The child's task is to listen carefully and answer these questions, demonstrating an enhanced ability to focus on and understand the auditory information amid potential distractions.

Scoring Criteria:

- Each correctly answered question earns 1 mark.

- Total marks for this task: 10 (10 questions x 1 mark each)

- Scoring 60% and above: Satisfactory performance, successful completion of Level 2

- Scoring below 60%: Needs further practice and remediation

This Level 2 assessment aims to test the child's advanced auditory processing skills, including the ability to focus on complex spoken information and make inferences based on the narrative. Success in this task indicates a higher level of auditory figure-ground perception and comprehension skills.

Summer is all about great weather, good company and great food. There is nothing quite like enjoying a good meal with a cold drink, listening to music with friends and feeling the grass in between your toes while you soak up some sun. Bank holidays in the United Kingdom generally fall on a Monday, which means that everyone gets to enjoy a three-day relaxing weekend. In the summer, if the weather is warm and the sun is shining, friends and family gather and have what the British and Australians call a "Barbie", a short form of the word barbeque, in their backyard, park or on the beach. Children get the chance to run around and play while the adults cook the food, drink and have a good chat. There is no doubt that meat and chicken that is cooked on a grill with charcoal outside, tastes much better than meat that is cooked in a traditional cooker or oven. The aroma itself is mouth-watering and is much healthier too. On the menu you will find grilled steak, chicken legs, chops, hamburgers and bangers. A seasonal salad, potato salads, corn and coleslaw are the nations favourite side dishes that go well with a barbeque. Trifle, cheesecake and fruit salads are popular foods for summer barbecue gatherings.

Answer the following in full sentences:

1. What is a barbie? ____
2. Where do people have a barbie? _______________________________________
3. What do people cook on a barbeque? _______________________________________
4. What are the traditional side dishes? _______________________________________
5. What do people usually have for dessert? _______________________________________

Circle (True) or (False). And then correct all mistakes:

1. Bank holidays usually fall on a Friday.	True	False
2. Barbeques only happen in gardens.	True	False
3. Children have a fun time.	True	False
4. Barbeques are healthier than ovens.	True	False
5. Chicken is only used on a barbeque.	True	False

Auditory Discrimination Assessment - Level 1

Auditory Discrimination: This ability allows an individual to recognize, compare, and differentiate between distinct sounds. It's essential for understanding that similar-sounding words, such as "forty" and "fourteen," are different.

These rubrics evaluate the child's ability to discern subtle differences in sounds—a critical skill for effective communication and language development. Achieving a satisfactory score in Level 1 is necessary to proceed to the more challenging Level 2, which further assesses the child's proficiency in auditory discrimination. Regular assessment and targeted remediation can enhance this skill, aiding in the child's overall auditory processing and understanding.

Task: Sound Identification Activity

Instructions:

1. Prepare a sound-making area where various sounds can be produced behind a screen or board, hidden from the child's view.

2. Introduce the activity to the child, explaining that they will hear different sounds and their task is to identify each sound based on hearing alone.

3. Produce a series of distinct sounds, one at a time, from behind the screen or board. Use everyday objects or actions to create these sounds.

Suggested Sounds for the Activity:

- Clapping hands

- Tearing a piece of paper

- Cutting paper with scissors

- Bouncing a ball

- Snapping fingers

- Clicking a camera

- Popping a balloon

- Stapling a paper

Scoring Criteria:

- Each correctly identified sound earns 2 marks.

- Total marks for this task: Varies depending on the number of sounds used (e.g., 8 sounds x 2 marks each = 16 marks)

- Scoring 60% and above: Satisfactory performance, eligible to move to Level 2

- Scoring below 60%:   Needs further practice and remediation

This Level 1 assessment is designed to evaluate the child's basic auditory discrimination skills.   The ability to distinguish between different sounds is crucial for language development and auditory processing.   This activity also adds an element of fun, encouraging active listening in a playful context.

Auditory Discrimination Assessment - Level 2

Task: Match and Reason Sound Containers

Instructions:

1. Prepare several small containers (like old film containers or small plastic bottles) that have been cleaned. Ensure they are opaque or covered with paper if transparent.

2. Fill two of each type of container with the same items (e.g., rice, beans, stones) to the same level, creating pairs that make the same sound when shaken. Seal the lids with hot glue for safety.

3. Mix up the containers and present them to the child.

4. The child's task is to shake each container, listen to the sound it makes, and then try to find its matching pair based only on the sound.

5. After the child selects a pair, ask them to explain why they think the two containers match, focusing on their auditory discrimination and reasoning skills.

Scoring Criteria:

- Each correctly matched pair of containers earns 2 marks.

- Total marks for this task: Depends on the number of container pairs (e.g., 5 pairs x 2 marks each = 10 marks)

- Scoring 60% and above: Satisfactory performance, successful completion of Level 2

- Scoring below 60%:   Needs further practice and remediation

This Level 2 assessment tests the child's advanced auditory discrimination skills.   It challenges them not only to distinguish between different sounds but also to reason and articulate their thought process in matching sounds. This activity enhances critical listening and cognitive skills, as well as encourages the development of verbal expression in explaining their choices.

Auditory Blending Assessment - Level 1

Auditory Blending: The ability to synthesize individual sounds (phonemes) of a word to recognize the word as a whole.

These rubrics assess a child's proficiency in combining phonemes to form complete words. Achieving a satisfactory score in Level 1 indicates readiness for more advanced phonemic synthesis challenges in Level 2. This skill is a foundational component of literacy, and regular assessment with appropriate remediation can significantly aid in a child's reading development.

Task: Color and Complete Words Based on Sound Blends

Instructions:

1. Present the child with a series of pictures, each representing a simple word.

2. Alongside each picture, write the initial sounds (phonemes) of the word, leaving a blank for the child to fill in.

3. The child's task is to first color the picture and then listen as you say the individual sounds (phonemes) aloud.

4. The child must blend these sounds together to form a word, recognize what the word is (based on the picture),

and write the correct letters in the blanks to complete the word.

Scoring Criteria:

- Each correctly completed word earns 1 mark.

- Total marks for this task: 10 (10 words x 1 mark each)

- Scoring 60% and above: Satisfactory performance, eligible to move to Level 2

- Scoring below 60%: Needs further practice and remediation

This Level 1 assessment is designed to evaluate the child's basic auditory blending skills. It tests their ability to synthesize individual sounds into whole words, a fundamental skill for reading and phonemic awareness. This task also includes a visual element (coloring the picture), which aids in word recognition and adds an engaging aspect to the activity.

Auditory Blending Assessment - Level 2

Task: Complete Words with Correct 'S' Blends

Instructions:

1. Present the child with a series of incomplete words that require an 'S' blend to be completed. Each word should start with a blank space for the 'S' blend.

2. Provide a box containing various 'S' blends (like 'st,' 'sp,' 'sn,' 'sl,' 'sc,' etc.).

3. The child's task is to select the correct 'S' blend from the box and complete each word.

Scoring Criteria:

- Each correctly completed word earns 1 mark.

- Total marks for this task: 10 (10 words x 1 mark each)

- Scoring 60% and above: Satisfactory performance, successful completion of Level 2

- Scoring below 60%: Needs further practice and remediation

This Level 2 assessment is designed to test the child's advanced auditory blending skills, specifically focusing on their ability to recognize and use 'S' blends in words. This task requires the child to not only blend sounds but also to understand and apply more complex phonetic structures, which is crucial for reading and phonological processing.

st	sp	sh	sn	st	sw	sp	sl

 …………..ake	 …………..oon
 …………..oes	…………..own
 ……...rawberry	 …………..ar
…………..an	 …………..irt
 …………..ain	 …………..ider

Auditory Closure Assessment - Level 1

Auditory Closure: The skill of auditory closure involves the ability to combine sounds into words, even if the whole word isn't clearly articulated. This includes understanding words when parts of them are obscured by noise or when they're spoken quickly.

These rubrics aim to assess a child's ability to recognize and understand words when certain sounds may be missing or unclear. Successfully completing Level 1 is necessary before moving on to the more challenging Level 2, ensuring the child is prepared for advanced auditory closure tasks. Regular assessment and appropriate remediation are key to enhancing this auditory processing skill.

Task: Complete the Sentences

Instructions:

1. Present the child with a series of short sentences. Each sentence should be incomplete, with a key word or part of a word missing.

2. The child's task is to read the sentences aloud and use their understanding of the sentence context to fill in the missing parts.

Scoring Criteria:

- Each correctly completed sentence earns 2 marks.

- Total marks for this task: 8 (4 sentences x 2 marks each)

- Scoring 60% and above: Satisfactory performance, eligible to move to Level 2

- Scoring below 60%: Needs further practice and remediation

This Level 1 assessment aims to evaluate the child's basic auditory closure skills. It tests their ability to comprehend incomplete auditory information and use context to make logical conclusions. This skill is fundamental for effective listening and communication, especially in situations where speech is distorted or incomplete.

I forgot to bring my math book home from school so I can't to my _____

A. Homework
B. Craft project
C. Video game

My sister woke up with a high fever today. My mom made her a

_____

appointment.

A. Veterinary
B. Doctor's
C. Library

My brother didn't eat his dinner last night, so he woke up this morning feeling very ____.

A. Hungry
B. Tired
C. Hurt

I fell and scraped my knee. My mom cleaned my boo, boo and put a ____ on it.

A. Scratch
B. Band aid
C. Sticker

Auditory Closure Assessment - Level 2

Task: Expand the Gingerbread House Story

Instructions:

1. Read aloud a portion of the "Gingerbread House" story to the child. This portion should end at a suspenseful or critical point, leaving the story obviously incomplete.

2. After reading, encourage the child to use their imagination to continue or complete the story. This can be done either verbally or through writing, depending on the child's comfort level and abilities.

Scoring Criteria:

- Assess the child's response for creativity, coherence, and how well it connects with the original story fragment.

- Consider awarding points for imaginative ideas, logical story progression, and effective closure of the story.

- Total marks for this task: Based on a qualitative assessment of the child's response.

Note: Since this task is more about creative expression and less about right or wrong answers, scoring can be subjective. Emphasize the child's effort and creativity.

This Level 2 assessment is designed to test the child's auditory closure skills at a more advanced level. It encourages imaginative thinking and the ability to create a coherent continuation of a story based on an incomplete narrative. This activity not only assesses auditory processing but also stimulates creative thinking and storytelling abilities.

Our Gingerbread House

One year my family made a large gingerbread house. First we glued it together with frosting. We carefully placed it on a piece of cardboard for its yard. Next we decorated it with candy. My brother put mints all over the roof. My sister put licorice next to the door. I made trees out of green M&M's. My father put a wreath made of candy on the door. My mother put four red candies on each corner of the yard. Our gingerbread house turned out perfect!

Imagine you had a gingerbread house. Tell how you would decorate it.

Auditory Sequential Memory Assessment - Level 1

Auditory Sequential Memory: The ability to recall the sequence of sounds in words, recognizing which sounds come first, middle, and last. This skill is crucial for segmenting words into their component sounds, a foundational aspect of learning to read and spell.

These rubrics are designed to evaluate a child's proficiency in auditory sequential memory. A satisfactory score in Level 1 indicates that the child is ready for the increased challenge of Level 2. Regular assessment and targeted remediation help enhance this crucial auditory skill, supporting the child's reading and spelling abilities.

Task: Remember and Recall a Series of Items or Numbers

Instructions:

1. Read aloud a short sequence of items or numbers to the child. The sequence should be age-appropriate and not too long, ideally consisting of 3-5 items or numbers.

2. After reading the sequence once, ask the child to repeat it back to you in the exact order it was presented.

Scoring Criteria:

- Award 2 marks for each correctly recalled item in the correct order.

- Total marks for this task: Based on the number of items in the sequence (e.g., 5 items x 2 marks each = 10 marks)

- Scoring 60% and above: Satisfactory performance, eligible to move to Level 2

- Scoring below 60%: Needs further practice and remediation

This Level 1 assessment is designed to evaluate the child's basic auditory sequential memory skills, assessing their ability to process, store, and recall auditory information in the correct order. This foundational skill is crucial for following directions, comprehension, and learning.

Read the story then choose the correct answer for each question.

Independence Day

My name is Jan. I love Independence Day. Independence Day is on August 31st every year. My mummy takes me to see the parade. We go to the savannah to see the parade. We hold small flags in our hands. We wave the flags at the marchers. I like the horses best.

Choose the correct answers.

1. Who loves Independence Day?
   a. Jan   b. Mummy

2. What does she like best?
   a. the flags   b. the horses

3. When is Independence Day celebrated?
   a. August 1st b. August 31st

4. Where do they go to see the parade?
   a. the street   b. the savannah

5. What do they do with the flags?
   a. wave   b. hide

Auditory Sequential Memory Assessment - Level 2

Task: Answer Questions Based on Sequences

Instructions:

1. Read aloud a more complex sequence of information to the child. This could be a short story, a list of instructions, or a series of events.

2. After reading, ask the child a series of questions based on the sequence to test their memory of the details and the order in which they occurred.

Scoring Criteria:

- Each correctly answered question earns 2 marks.

- Total marks for this task: Varies based on the number of questions (e.g., 4 questions x 2 marks each = 8 marks)

- Scoring 60% and above: Satisfactory performance, successful completion of Level 2

- Scoring below 60%: Needs further practice and remediation

This Level 2 assessment aims to test and enhance the child's ability to remember and recall information presented in a sequence, focusing on more complex auditory processing and memory recall skills. It helps in assessing the child's ability to listen, comprehend, and recall details in a specific order, which is crucial for advanced learning and understanding.

Read the text carefully:

My class is taking a field trip to a campground next week. I am very excited because we are going to learn how to <u>pitch</u> a tent. If the weather is nice and cool, we can even start a camp fire and roast some marshmallows. We will leave for the trip at 8 A.M and get to the campsite by 10 A.M.

I have a new book to read on the bus about the natural <u>heritage</u>. I prepared a gym bag with all the things that I would need: a flashlight, a sleeping bag, a knife, and some dried food.

Our teacher will show us how to identify poisonous animals and plants in the woods. The trip will teach us about nature and what it is like to live without many things from the modern world.

Answer the following questions:

1. Where the class field trip is is going to be to?

____

____

2. Why is the boy excited to be on this trip?

____

____

3. What are the items that the boy prepared to take with him?

____

____

4. How much time does the way take to reach the campsite?

____

INFORMAL ASSESSMENT (LANGUAGE)

Receptive and expressive language are two key components of communication skills. They represent different aspects of how we understand and use language in our daily interactions.

Receptive Language:

- **Definition:** Receptive language refers to the ability to understand or comprehend language. It involves the processing and interpretation of information that is received, either through listening or reading.

- **Examples:**

  - Understanding what others say during conversation.

  - Comprehending stories read from a book.

  - Following instructions or directions given by others.

  - Interpreting body language and facial expressions.

- **Development:** Begins very early in life, as babies start by understanding tone, then words, and eventually sentences and complex instructions.

Expressive Language:

- **Definition:** Expressive language is about how an individual communicates their thoughts, ideas, and feelings. It encompasses the use of words, sentences, gestures, and writing to convey messages to others.

- Examples:

  - Speaking, ranging from babbling in babies to complex speech in adults.

  - Writing text or messages.

  - Using sign language or other forms of non-verbal communication like facial expressions or body language to express ideas.

  - Storytelling or describing events or experiences.

- Development: Develops as children learn to babble, form words, create sentences, and engage in conversations. It continues to evolve throughout life as individuals learn new words and ways to express themselves.

In essence, receptive language is about intake and understanding of information, while expressive language is about output or how one communicates their thoughts. Both are crucial for effective communication and often develop together, though it's not uncommon for individuals, especially children, to have different levels of proficiency in each.

Receptive Language Assessment - Level 1

Task: Basic Reading Comprehension

Instructions:

1. Provide the child with a short, simple written passage. This could be a brief story, a description, or a series of simple statements. The content should be straightforward and within the child's reading level.

2. After the child has read the passage, ask a series of questions based on the content. These questions should focus on basic comprehension, such as identifying the main idea, simple details, and the sequence of events.

Scoring Criteria:

- Each correctly answered question earns 2 marks.

- Total marks for this task: Typically, 10 (5 questions x 2 marks each)

- Scoring 60% and above: Satisfactory performance, eligible to move to Level 2

- Scoring below 60%: Needs further practice and remediation

This Level 1 assessment is designed to evaluate the child's basic receptive language skills in reading. It tests their ability to read and comprehend simple written material, an essential skill for language development and early literacy.

What If....?

Read the story below.

Nandi sat on the blue steps of her house. She was wondering..... What if jelly beans made you jump really high? You could get to school in one big leap!

What if houses were rocket ships? Your family could go holidays to the moon! What if the pictures in books flew around your head when Dad read to you? What if my pink gumboots were magical? I could run faster than my big brother! "Nandi, what are you doing?"Asked Nandi's big brother. Nandi sat back on the step with a big smile on her face. "Just wondering," she said.

Answer each question.

1. What Nandi was wondering about the jelly beans?

   ____

2. What do you wonder when Dad read to you?

   ____

3. Why did Nandi think that her pink gumboots were magical?

   ____

4. "Nandi what are you doing?" Who said that?

   a.   Mum   b. Big brother   c. Dad

5. What if the flowers could talk? What would they say?

   ____

Receptive Language Assessment - Level 2

Task: Advanced Reading Comprehension

Instructions:

1. Provide the child with a written passage that is more complex than the one used in Level 1. This should include longer narratives, more intricate language, or more detailed content, suitable for the child's age but providing a challenge.

2. After the child has read the passage, ask a series of questions that require a deeper understanding, critical thinking, and inference. These questions should test the child's ability to comprehend subtleties, infer meanings, and understand the sequence and implications of events.

Scoring Criteria:

- Each correctly answered question earns 2 marks.

- Total marks for this task: Typically, 10 (5 questions x 2 marks each)

- Scoring 60% and above: Satisfactory performance, successful completion of Level 2

- Scoring below 60%: Needs further practice and remediation

This Level 2 assessment aims to test the child's advanced receptive language skills in reading. It evaluates their ability to understand complex written information, make inferences, and draw conclusions based on the text, all of which are crucial for higher-level reading comprehension and academic success.

Q. Reading Comprehension

Anna's lute

Anna's favorite hobby is playing lute. She spends a lot of her free time playing lute. She started learning to play lute when she was 5 years old. She played in her school's band.

Anna's dad bought her a lute and she started practicing every day after school. It was very loud, but her mother never complained. She improved a lot, and playing lute has been her favorite hobby ever since.

1) What is Anna's favorite hobby?

____

2) When did Anna start to play lute?

____

3) Who bought Anna a lute?

____

4) What is the title of the story?

____

5) Where did Anna perform lute?

____

Expressive Language Assessment - Level 1

Task: Basic Oral Expression

Instructions:

1. Engage the child in a simple conversation or ask them to describe familiar objects, experiences, or events. The topics should be relatable and easy for the child to talk about.

2. Prompt the child with open-ended questions or simple topics to encourage them to speak.

3. Listen to the child's responses, noting their ability to form coherent sentences, use appropriate vocabulary, and stay on topic.

Scoring Criteria:

- Award points for clear articulation, appropriate use of vocabulary, sentence structure, and staying on topic.

- Each topic or question can be scored out of 1 mark.

- Total marks for this task: Typically, 10 (10 topics/questions x 1 mark each)

- Scoring 60% and above: Satisfactory performance, eligible to move to Level 2

- Scoring below 60%: Needs further practice and remediation

This Level 1 assessment is designed to evaluate the child's basic expressive language skills, focusing on their ability to communicate verbally. It assesses clarity of speech, vocabulary usage, sentence formation, and the ability to convey ideas or experiences effectively.

Unscramble and write the word to complete the sentence.

1. gyeren    Healthy food gives me ____________.

2. stuifr    Bananas and apples are____________.

3. ymg    I like to exercise at the ____________.

4. eelf regat    I ______________ today.

5. ssldaa    I like to have __________ for lunch.

6. nimsitav    Fruits a vegetables have lots of____________.

7. talbesvege    Eat your ______________!

8. gnicora oodsf   ______________ are very healthy.

9. knuj ofdo    I used to eat lots of __________.

10. Leef yrghnu    I ______________. Let's eat!

Expressive Language Assessment - Level 2

Task: Advanced Oral Expression

Instructions:

1. Engage the child in a conversation that requires a higher level of thinking, such as discussing hypothetical situations, expressing opinions on various topics, or narrating a story they create.

2. Ask open-ended questions that encourage the child to elaborate on their ideas, use descriptive language, and structure their thoughts coherently.

3. Evaluate the child's responses, focusing on their ability to use complex sentence structures, varied vocabulary, clarity in expressing abstract or non-concrete ideas, and their overall communicative competence.

Scoring Criteria:

- Points should be awarded for advanced language use (vocabulary and sentence structure), clarity of expression, creativity, and ability to construct and convey complex ideas.

- Each topic or question can be scored out of 1 mark.

- Total marks for this task: Typically, 8 (8 topics/questions x 1 mark each)

- Scoring 60% and above: Satisfactory performance, successful completion of Level 2

- Scoring below 60%:   Needs further practice and remediation

This Level 2 assessment is designed to evaluate the child's advanced expressive language skills. It tests their ability to articulate more complex thoughts and ideas, use language creatively, and engage in more abstract or sophisticated verbal communication. This level assesses not just the linguistic ability but also the cognitive aspects of language use.

I help at home

Grammar.
Read the sentences and fill in the gaps with a pronoun, verb to be or a noun.

1   She is .... the mirror
2   He is taking out the ....
3   She is .... the floor
4   They .... washing up the dishes
5   .... is feeding the dog
6   He is .... the toilet
7   She is ....
8   He .... doing the laundry

Vocabulary.
Rearrange the letters to find out the word.

1 ROOMB ....   3 VENO ....
2 NAPTUDS ....   4 UUCMVA NEARCLE ....

GRAPHOMOTOR SKILLS ASSESSMENT

Graphomotor Skills:

Graphomotor skills are essential for a child to write effectively. A deficiency in these skills represents a disconnect between a child's thoughts and the ability to transcribe them onto paper compellingly for readers.

Children with graphomotor difficulties are often mistakenly labeled as lazy or unmotivated because they may hesitate to produce written work. Such children might develop an aversion to school and become disengaged. Indicators of poor graphomotor function can include struggles with tasks requiring fine motor skills, such as cutting food, assembling puzzles, or manipulating small objects. An unusual or awkward pen grip can also signal graphomotor skill issues.

Five key skill areas associated with graphomotor abilities include:

1. **Visual Perceptual Skills:** The capacity to visually perceive a letter or word, understand its meaning, or judge its accuracy.

2.   Orthographic Coding: The ability to store written words or letters in memory and retrieve them as needed.

3. Kinesthetic Feedback: The awareness of where body parts are in space, which is necessary for executing motor movements.

4. Motor Planning and Execution (Praxis): The process of planning and executing motor actions.

5. Visual-Motor Coordination: The coordination of visual perception and motor movement, allowing for the accurate reproduction of visual material.

Understanding and developing these skills are crucial for children's writing development. Targeted support and intervention can enhance these abilities, allowing children to express their ideas effectively through writing.

<u>Below is the sample of a class 4 child's writing who has graphic motor issues:-</u>

Assessment of Graphomotor Skills

When evaluating graphomotor skills, it's crucial to account for several factors that can impact a child's ability to write. These include:

1. Prerequisite Skills for Handwriting:

- **Scribbling:** Observe the child's initial attempts at writing to assess control and comfort with a writing instrument.

- **Identifying Shapes:** Ensure the child can recognize and reproduce basic shapes as a foundation for letter formation.

- **Recognizing Likeness and Differences:** Check the child's ability to discern and replicate differences in visual items.

- **Eye-Hand Coordination:** Assess how well the child's vision guides their hand movements, an essential skill for writing.

- **Cutting and Pasting:** Evaluate the child's precision in cutting and pasting within designated spaces, indicating fine motor control.

2. Observing the Child's Posture:

- **Back Position:** The child should sit with their back erect, supporting a stable writing posture.

- **Shoulders:** Shoulders should be relaxed with a slight forward bend, allowing free arm movement.

- **Head Distance:** The child's head should be at an appropriate distance from the paper to avoid strain and provide a clear view of their writing.

3. Paper Positioning:

- For right-handed children, tilting the paper to the left can facilitate a more natural writing motion.

- For left-handed children, tilting the paper to the right is usually more comfortable and effective.

These considerations are essential for a comprehensive assessment of a child's graphomotor skills. By observing these elements, you can identify areas where the child may need additional support and intervention to improve their writing abilities.

Efficient Pencil Grasp

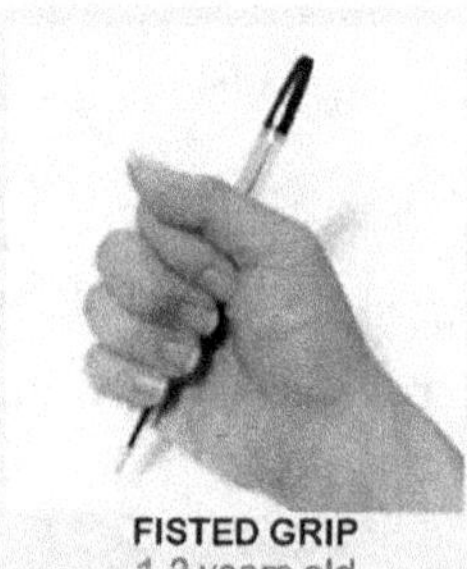

FISTED GRIP
1-2 years old

Children often hold their writing tool like a dagger, scribbling using their whole arm.

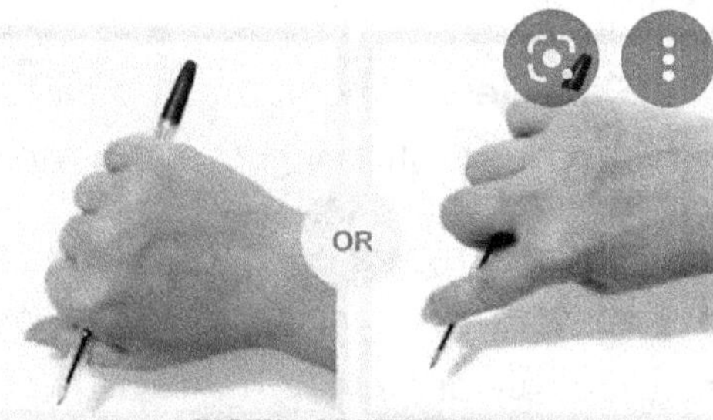

DIGITAL PRONATE GRIP
2-3 years old

All fingers are holding the writing tool but the wrist is turned so that the palm is facing down towards the page. Movement now comes mostly from the elbow. Children should start being able to copy a horizontal, vertical and circular line.

4 FINGER GRIP
3-4 years old

4 fingers are held on the writing tool. Movement is mostly from the wrist and the hand and fingers move as one.

STATIC TRIPOD GRIP
4-6 years old

This is a 3 finger grasp, where the thumb, index finger and middle finger work as one unit.

DYNAMIC TRIPOD GRIP
By 6 or 7 years old

Using only 3 fingers to hold the writing tool. This isthe ideal grip to help move the pencil efficiently, accurately.

MATHEMATICAL ASSESSMENT

Mathematical Calculations: A Complex Skill Set

Mathematical calculations encompass a complex system of skills, concepts, and processes. Mastery in mathematics depends on the interplay of numerous abilities and cognitive mechanisms. Difficulties in learning math are prevalent and significant, necessitating dedicated instructional efforts in both mainstream and special education.

Students struggling with math may experience a range of issues. Common challenges include trouble with the quick recall of basic arithmetic facts and consistency in executing written computations. These difficulties can vary from mild to severe and may present themselves in diverse ways.

The impact of persistent difficulties in math can lead to students withdrawing effort, suffering from diminished self-esteem, and exhibiting avoidance behaviors. As special educators, it's imperative to recognize the gravity of these issues. There is much that can and must be done to address these learning challenges, which deserve far more attention than they have typically received. Ensuring that students with math learning problems receive the support they need is essential for their academic and personal development.

Math Assessment - Level 1

Task: Basic Arithmetic and Number Skills

Instructions:

1. Prepare a series of simple math problems or exercises. These should be appropriate for the child's age and educational level, focusing on basic concepts.

2. Include a variety of tasks, such as number recognition, basic counting, simple addition and subtraction, and identification of basic shapes.

3. Present these tasks to the child either verbally, written, or with visual aids, depending on their learning preference.

Scoring Criteria:

- Each correct answer earns 2 marks.

- Total marks for this task: Varies depending on the number of questions (e.g., 5 questions = 10 marks).

- Scoring 60% and above: Satisfactory performance, eligible to move to Level 2.

- Scoring below 60%: Needs further practice and remediation.

This Level 1 math assessment is designed to evaluate the child's basic understanding of foundational math concepts. The focus is on their ability to perform simple calculations, recognize numbers, and understand basic mathematical principles.

Write the number name:		2. Write the number numeral:	
130		One hundred and thirty-two	
133		One hundred and thirty-four	
135		One hundred and thirty-six	

2. Complete the sums:

130 + 1 =	100 + ___ = 133	130 + ___ = 137	139 - 9 =
130 + 3 =	100 + ___ = 134	130 + ___ = 139	137 - 7 =
130 + 5 =	100 + ___ = 136	130 + ___ = 132	135 - 30 =

3. Fill in the missing numbers:

140		142		144				

4. Decompose (breaking up numbers)

___ + ___ = 135	500+80+3 =	8+40+300=	___ + ___ =364

5. Write the following numbers from smallest to biggest.

125	135	185	205	115	155	215	145	165	375

Math Assessment - Level 2

Task: Intermediate Arithmetic and Problem-Solving

Instructions:

1. Prepare a series of math problems or exercises that are more challenging than Level 1. These should be suitable for the child's age and educational development but provide a slightly higher level of difficulty.

2. Include a variety of tasks, such as larger addition and subtraction problems, basic multiplication and division, understanding place values, and solving simple word problems.

3. Present these tasks to the child either in written form or verbally, depending on their learning preference.

Scoring Criteria:

- Each correct answer earns 2 marks.

- Total marks for this task: Varies depending on the number of questions (e.g., 5 questions = 10 marks).

- Scoring 60% and above: Satisfactory performance, successful completion of Level 2.

- Scoring below 60%: Needs further practice and remediation.

This Level 2 math assessment is designed to test the child's ability to handle more complex arithmetic operations and to apply mathematical concepts in different contexts. It also begins to evaluate the child's problem-solving skills and understanding of mathematical relationships.

Describe, compare and arrange numbers.

1. Fill in the missing numbers. [9]

_____; 233	299; _____; 301	150; _____
_____; 176	124; _____; 126	366; _____
_____; 350	282; _____; 284	215; _____

2. Order the numbers in descending order. [2]

312; 123; 231	_________; _________; _________.
236; 241; 243	_________; _________; _________.

3. Arrange the series of numbers in ascending order. [2]

119; 291; 109	_________; _________; _________.
256; 146; 386	_________; _________; _________.

4. Complete the table. [4]

Double the numbers		Halve the numbers	
15 →	24 →	18 →	50 →

5. Complete: More / less than. [4]

5 more than 346 = _______	10 less than 174 = _______
4 less than 233 = _______	3 more than 378 = _______

Place Value Worksheet - Level 1

Objective: Understand the value of each digit in a number based on its place (ones, tens, hundreds).

Instructions: Below are some numbers. Write the value of each digit according to its place in the number. Then, write the expanded form of the number.

This worksheet aims to build a foundational understanding of place value, helping children recognize how each digit in a number has a different value depending on its position. The bonus challenge questions further reinforce this understanding by applying the concept in different contexts.

4 - Digit Place Value Worksheet

Write the 4-digit number based on the given place values

1. _____ = 2,000 + 400 + 70 + 3

2. _____ = 8,000 + 600 + 40 + 4

3. _____ = 6,000 + 900 + 50 + 1

4. _____ = 2,000 + 900 + 60 + 2

5. _____ = 9,000 + 60

6. _____ = 6,000 + 100 + 40

7. _____ = 7,000 + 500 + 80 + 9

8. _____ = 1,000 + 800 + 90 + 1

9. _____ = 5,000 + 600 + 60 + 6

10. _____ = 3,000 + 600 + 30 + 2

Place Value Worksheet - Level 2

Objective: Deepen understanding of place value for larger numbers and perform basic operations based on place value.

Instructions: Below are some numbers. Identify the value of each digit according to its place. Then, write the expanded form of the number. Complete the additional tasks based on place value.

This Level 2 worksheet is designed to challenge students' understanding of place value in larger numbers and apply this understanding in various contexts, including ordering, comparing, and basic arithmetic operations based on place value. The bonus challenges offer additional opportunities to apply place value knowledge in different ways.

5-Digit Place Value Worksheet

The 5-digit number 62755 can be expanded in the form
60000 + 2000 + 700 + 50 + 5. That is,

62755 = 60000 + 2000 + 700 + 50 + 5

Write the 5-digit number in the blank space given.

1   40,000 + 300 + 7 = _______________________

2   90,000 + 6,000 + 60 + 4 = _______________

3   30,000 + 5,000 + 700 + 60 + 1 = ___________

4   40,000 + 8,000 + 600 + 60 + 4 = ___________

5   90,000 + 5,000 + 300 + 80 + 2 = ___________

Logical and Reasoning Worksheet - Level 1

Objective: Develop basic logical reasoning and problem-solving skills.

Instructions: Complete the following activities that test your ability to identify patterns, relationships, and solve simple problems.

This worksheet aims to introduce children to the basics of logical thinking and reasoning. The tasks are designed to be straightforward yet engaging, helping them understand patterns, relationships, sequences, and basic cause and effect. The bonus challenges add a slightly more complex dimension to the assessment, testing their ability to continue patterns and perform simple arithmetic.

Complete the following:

1) 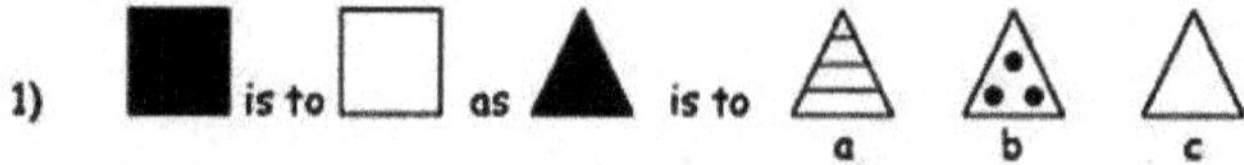 is to ▢ as ▲ is to (a) (b) (c)

2) is to as is to (a) (b) (c)

3) is to as is to (a) (b) (c)

4) is to as is to (a) (b) (c)

5) is to as is to (a) (b) (c)

Logical and Reasoning Worksheet - Level 2

Objective: Enhance logical reasoning skills and problem-solving abilities with more complex tasks.

Instructions: Complete the following activities that test your ability to analyze information, identify more complex patterns, relationships, and solve problems.

This Level 2 worksheet is designed to challenge students further in their logical thinking and reasoning capabilities. The tasks are more complex, requiring students to think abstractly, solve problems with multiple steps, and understand more intricate relationships and patterns. The bonus challenges are aimed at testing their ability to apply these skills in less straightforward scenarios.

The blank square in the first five boxes needs to be filled by one of the patterns in the second five boxes. Circle the correct letter.

Example

A   B   C   D   E

1.

A   B   C   D   E

2.

A   B   C   D   E

3.

A   B   C   D   E

4.

A   B   C   D   E

5.

A   B   C   D   E

HOME REMEDIAL PLAN

SPECIFIC LEARNING DISORDER

Embracing Learning and Thinking Differences

Learning and thinking differences are a normal part of childhood; every child has their own set of strengths and challenges. Parents are encouraged to identify and nurture their children's strengths, whether they lie in dance, music, sports, art, computers, or playing an instrument. It's important to regularly celebrate your child's successes in these areas.

Children may feel frustrated or become withdrawn due to learning differences or the typical challenges of growing up. Support your child with love and understanding, acknowledging that their unique way of learning is just that—unique, not indicative of intelligence. Many individuals with learning differences are exceptionally bright and go on to achieve great success.

Colleges often have programs to support students with diverse learning and thinking styles, helping them earn degrees in their chosen fields. Specialists, such as reading and math tutors, can offer strategies to bolster academic skills. Parents can further aid their children's organization by using alarms, writing instructions clearly, and placing visual reminders around the home. Mind mapping with graphic organizers can be an effective tool for comprehending entire subject chapters.

Parents should also explore the resources available through their child's school special education department. Accommodations might include additional time for assessments, seating arrangements that minimize distractions, proximity to the teacher to enhance focus, and a buddy system for consistent task reminders. These supports can make a significant difference in a child's educational journey.

INDIVIDUAL EDUCATION PROGRAM

<u>Individual Education Program (IEP) in Indian Schools</u>

Indian government and public schools are required to provide an Individual Education Program (IEP) for students identified with certain learning disabilities. The IEP sets both short-term and annual learning goals, tailored to each student's unique needs.

The IEP serves as a collaborative effort, bringing together teachers, parents, school administrators, and related service providers. Its aim is to enhance educational outcomes for children with disabilities. The program is central to delivering quality education, setting measurable yearly objectives, and establishing realistic educational expectations.

An IEP typically includes necessary educational accommodations and modifications to facilitate a child's success. These supports are often divided into two categories:

1. **Accommodations:** These may consist of extended time for assignments or tests, seating arrangements close to the teacher to aid focus, or the use of assistive technology such as computer applications for writing, calculators for math, or audiobooks for reading.

2. **Modifications:** Based on recommendations from medical professionals, modifications might include medication for managing mental health concerns like depression or anxiety. Furthermore, if assessments by psychologists and special educators reveal below-average IQ, curriculum modifications can be implemented to simplify learning.

The IEP's goal is to create a supportive and adaptive educational environment, ensuring that every child with a disability has access to an effective and personalized learning experience.

EPILOGUE

As we reach the closing pages of this journey, I find myself reflecting on the myriad of emotions, experiences, and insights that have been shared. This book was not just a collection of chapters but a tapestry woven with the threads of resilience, hope, and unconditional love that define the world of special parenting.

In these stories and advice, there's a universal truth that resonates - every child is a unique universe of potential, and every parent a guardian of this universe. The journey of parenting a child with special needs is not just about overcoming challenges; it's about celebrating differences, embracing the unexpected, and finding joy in the smallest of achievements.

I hope that as you turned each page, you found not just information, but also comfort, inspiration, and a sense of community. Remember, you are not alone on this path. The collective wisdom and strength of all those who walk this journey with you are always there to light the way.

As you move forward, may you carry with you the courage, love, and wisdom from these pages. May they serve as a beacon of hope on the days when the journey gets tough, and a reminder of the joy and love that makes it all worthwhile.

Thank you for allowing me to be a part of your journey.

With heartfelt wishes for your continued strength and joy,

Dr. Kajal Suri

"Like the shared light of stars in the night sky, the wisdom in these pages grows brighter when passed from hand to hand. If you've found solace or strength in our journey together, consider sharing this book with others who might be walking a similar path."